KINGDOM COME

JOHN MARK HICKS & BOBBY VALENTINE

KINGDOM COME

Embracing the Spiritual Legacy of David Lipscomb and James Harding

LEAFWOOD
PUBLISHERS

KINGDOM COME

Embracing the Spiritual Legacy of James Harding and David Lipscomb

Published by Leafwood Publishers

ISBN 0-9767790-6-4
Printed in the United States of America

Cover Design by Rick Gibson

For information contact:
Leafwood Publishers, Abilene, Texas
1-877-816-4455 toll free
www.leafwoodpublishers.com

06 07 08 09 10 11 12 13 14 / 10 9 8 7 6 5 4 3 2 1

Dedication

In faith, hope and love we dedicate this book
about the past to the future of the kingdom of God
among the Churches of Christ.

We believe in the future of God's colony,
trust in his powerful Spirit to shape her
and love her for Christ's sake.

May the past help guide us securely
into the future.

CONTENTS

Preface 9

Abbreviations 11

1. Introducing a Spiritual Legacy: Foreigners at Home 13

Part I. Kingdom Dynamics: Divine Action 25

2. Shadows of the Second Coming: "Thy Kingdom Come" 27

3. God Still Works: Trusting God's Providence 43

4. Holy Spirit: God's Redemptive Presence in the World 59

Part II. Kingdom Spirituality: Four Means of Grace 75

5. Listening to God: Reading Scripture 79

6. Releasing the Oppressed: Fellowship as a Means of Grace 93

7. Communing with God: The Lord's Day and the Lord's Table 111

8. Crying for the Kingdom: The Privilege of Prayer 127

Part III. Kingdom Life: Free to Serve 143

9. The Prince of Peace: Pledging Allegiance to the Kingdom 145

10. No Creed But Christ: Freedom to Think and Speak 163

11. Shadows No More: Towards Cosmic Liberation 179

Afterword

12. The Road Not Traveled: Where Do We Go From Here? 193

Notes 199

PREFACE

Can anything good come out of 1906? That year represents the moment when the Stone-Campbell unity movement divided. That year the U. S. government formalized a rupture within the body of Christ.

1906 is symbolic of a deep division within the Stone-Campbell Movement that had been fomenting nationwide for the previous twenty years and in some instances forty years. The 1906 Census reported the existence of two groups—the Churches of Christ (with 159,658 members primarily in Tennessee, Texas, Alabama, Mississippi and Arkansas) and the Christian Church (with almost one million members primarily in the North and Midwest).

This year, 2006, is the one hundredth anniversary of that symbolic date. Everyone laments division and this anniversary reminds us of the laudable goal of unity and the failure of Christians to maintain it.

But can we say anything good about 1906?

This book recovers a piece of forgotten history from the first decade of the twentieth century. Some of the finest examples of kingdom living to be found among Churches of Christ are found in the midst of that heartbreaking year of division. The "best" of Churches of Christ in 1906 is represented by the life, thought and practice of David Lipscomb (1831-1917) and James A. Harding (1848-1922), despite the fact that Lipscomb and Harding participated in the conditions which resulted in division.

In 1906 Lipscomb was teaching at the Nashville Bible School (NBS) and editing the *Gospel Advocate* in Nashville, Tennessee, while James A. Harding was teaching at Potter Bible College (PBC) and co-editing *The Christian Leader and the Way* in Bowling Green, Kentucky. They were acknowledged leaders among Churches of Christ, especially east of the Mississippi.

Their kingdom theology and spirituality, we believe, provides the contemporary church with a way forward into the future. If Churches of Christ—and other parts of the Stone-Campbell Movement as well—would re-appropriate their kingdom themes and practices, we believe the church would more fully participate in the emerging kingdom of God which will one day fill the earth with divine righteousness.

We invite you to join us on this journey of discovery as we encourage the church to embrace the spiritual legacy of Lipscomb and Harding.

Many people have contributed to the production of this book. None of them, of course, are responsible for its final form except the authors, but it would be deficient in many ways without their help. The faculty members of the Bible and Ministry department of Lipscomb University read an early version and discussed it with us. Their comments were quite helpful and their direction improved our efforts considerably. We thank them for their time and work on our behalf. Others, like Greg Taylor, Monroe Hawley, and Daryl Miller, have read parts of the manuscript at various stages—and we offer them our thanks.

Also, we thank Jonathan Melton, John Mark's student assistant, for his detailed work in checking some of our footnotes and references—but any mistakes are our responsibility. We also thank Leonard Allen for his editorial assistance and his willingness to place this work before the reading public.

And, of course, we offer our grateful love to our families, especially our wives Pamella and Jennifer. Their patience and support means more to us than anything else in the world. Through their love, we experience the love of God in ever new ways.

We offer this book in the hope that it might contribute to the ongoing discussion within the church about its identity and future. Our identity is discipleship—following Jesus—and our future is the fullness of God's reign upon the earth. We pray that God may bless your reading.

ABBREVIATIONS

CG	David Lipscomb, *Civil Government: Its Origin, Mission, and Destiny and the Christian's Relation to It* (Nashville: McQuiddy Printing Company, 1913; reprint of 1889 ed. from articles originally published in 1866).
CL	*Christian Leader*
CLW	*Christian Leader and the Way*
FF	*Firm Foundation*
GA	*Gospel Advocate*
GH	*Gospel Herald*
KJV	King James Version
LM	*Living Message*
MH	*Millennial Harbinger*
NBS	Nashville Bible School
NBST	Nashville Bible School Tradition
NIV	New International Version
PBC	Potter Bible College
QA	David Lipscomb and E. G. Sewell, *Questions Answered by Lipscomb and Sewell*, ed. M. C. Kurfees (Nashville: McQuiddy Printing Co., 1921).
Q&A	David Lipscomb, *Queries and Answers*, ed. J.W. Shepherd, 5th ed. (Nashville: Gospel Advocate Co., 1963).
RQ	*Restoration Quarterly*
SS	Revised Version, *Salvation from Sin*, edited by J. W. Shepherd (Nashville, Tennessee: McQuiddy, 1913).
TEV	Today's English Version
TT	Texas Tradition
WW	*Word and Work*

ONE

INTRODUCING A SPIRITUAL LEGACY: FOREIGNERS AT HOME

We are foreigners, but this is our home. Does that make sense? It does. We are foreigners because we are not comfortable with this world, the present evil age. We are uncomfortable with the increasing number of poor; we are uncomfortable with war; we are uncomfortable with injustice; and we are uncomfortable with sin. This world—as it presently exists—is not our home. Our values are not the values of this world. We are aliens here.

But we are home. This world is our home. God intended it—this created reality—for our habitation. We were created to reign with God and care for his cosmos. This world is home—it was built to be shared with us.

But how can we be both foreigners and at home? How can we be aliens in our own homeland? We are refugees in this present evil age who seek to reclaim what has been lost. We seek to restore what God created—to live in the home that God created for us as God intended us to live; to live in *shalom* at home with God.

We presently live in a fallen world. It is enveloped in the darkness of the Satanic kingdom. We live in the illusory matrix of the kingdom of darkness. The powers of darkness maintain this illusion and daily reload that illusion in the hearts of people.

We, however, yearn for the coming kingdom of God. When God created the world, divine love saturated the cosmos. God loves his world and seeks community with his co-regents who are made in his image—humanity. God reigned over the cosmos through his human representatives. But humanity loaded a new program—they chose the serpent's illusion of power and autonomy.

"Kingdom Come" refers to the hopeful expectation that the kingdom of God will break into the world, defeat the present darkness, and transform this fallen cosmos into a new heaven and new earth. We pray "thy kingdom come" as we groan for the redemption of the kingdom of God reloaded.

This was the kingdom vision of David Lipscomb and James A. Harding—and their spiritual legacy, as the title of the book suggests. Their spiritual vision invites us to participate in the kingdom of God as it breaks into the present darkness. Lipscomb and Harding lived with a future-orientation—they yearned for the coming of God's kingdom in its fullness. They envisioned a kingdom reloaded where God would restore what he originally created by making this world heaven on earth. But this restoration is a progressive in-breaking. As disciples progressively follow Jesus and are made like him, the kingdom of God will defeat the powers that enslave and delude humanity.

Consequently, Harding described Christian existence in the fallen world as that of a "foreigner." We think he was correct. But he also knew that God would one day make this world his home and that God created the cosmos as our home. So, for now, we are "foreigners at home." When God reloads his kingdom in its fullness, we will be truly at home in this world and no longer foreigners.

Disciples, therefore, live both in anticipation of the fullness of the kingdom at the second coming of Jesus and in the present power of the Spirit as they participate in the in-breaking of that kingdom. God trains, disciples and empowers his people through the Spirit as they seek him through Scripture, service, assembly and prayer. Disciples give each other freedom, call for peace and live in hope.

The contemporary church needs to hear this message. Ironically the first decade of the twentieth century provides a way forward for the church of the first decade in the twenty-first century. The Churches of

Christ in the early twentieth century chose not to follow that path but now have the opportunity to re-appropriate it and move into the future with hope and anticipation. As we listen to the voices of the past, they can push us into the future.

OUR PRESENT QUANDARY

The Churches of Christ find themselves in a quandary. For the most part, we are historically blind. We don't know our history and our sense of spiritual heritage is distorted. On the one hand, some believe the Churches of Christ have been bereft of spiritual vigor since their emergence in the early twentieth century. The Churches of Christ seemed to concentrate solely on defending and preserving church forms that defined our relationship with God. These critics consequently have little respect for their spiritual heritage. They have jettisoned their heritage because they judged it wanting in spirituality. We often find this group disassociating themselves from Churches of Christ and seeking spirituality in the greener pastures of Evangelicalism. But what they seek is part of our forgotten past.

On the other hand, some find their spiritual identity in church practices. They believe this is their spiritual heritage. Their spiritual life is shaped by debates with "denominationalists." Their spiritual vigor is found in their exclusive identity as the one true church. They respect their spiritual heritage for the wrong reason or deny they have a heritage other than the Bible itself. Indeed, some will dismiss any discussion of our history or "tradition" as insignificant for their own spiritual journey. They read the Bible for themselves and think they read it without the glasses given to them by their spiritual ancestors. They declare themselves autonomous readers as if their "family of origin" has had no influence on them. They do not realize that they read the Bible with the lenses of the 1940s and 1950s Churches of Christ. But there is another set of lenses in our forgotten past.

We believe Churches of Christ have a vibrant and relevant spiritual heritage. It is a past we should neither reject nor ignore. It has been forgotten for too long. It provides both a historic and contemporary "third way." Historically, we are neither Catholic nor Protestant but rather a believers' church movement.[1] Lipscomb looked to the Anabaptists of the sixteenth century as models, and Harding found a kindred spirit in George Mueller of the Brethren Church. For them, as for others in the believers' church tradition, discipleship—following Jesus—was the key dimension of kingdom life in the present evil age.

In the contemporary landscape, a renewal of Lipscomb's and Harding's spirituality provides guidance for navigating the chaotic seas of postmodernity, the Emerging Church movement, and our own seeming spiritual inertia. Lipscomb and Harding were modernists in the sense that they drank deeply from the wells of the Enlightenment. They were modern people within a modern movement rooted in modern perspectives. Yet, there was something in their kingdom vision that critiqued the progress of modernity. Their vision was antagonistic toward modernity in significant ways—especially the in-breaking kingdom of God. Their spirituality has something to offer our postmodern situation. Just as N. T. Wright resonates with many in the Emerging Church movement and with many postmoderns, much of Lipscomb and Harding will resonate with them as well. Reclaiming the spirituality of Lipscomb and Harding may be a way forward for Churches of Christ in the contemporary world.

Spiritual inertia arises when we are comfortable with both our church and our world. Spiritual arrogance expresses itself in supreme confidence in our church forms which translates into the feeling that "we have arrived"—we have restored the church. It's a done deal. But, more dangerously, spiritual inertia develops when we are so comfortable with our place in the culture that we find it more infuriating to critique presidential policy than to critique our wealth. We have become too comfortable with our ecclesial forms and our socio-economic location in society. We have lost the spiritual edge that was so much a part of Lipscomb's and Harding's kingdom vision.

We commend to the church the kingdom vision of Lipscomb and Harding as a way of negotiating between the relativities of postmodern spirituality and the arrogance of our modern church heritage. We believe it is a "third way"—a way forward, a way to embrace the kingdom of God in the present.

THE NASHVILLE BIBLE SCHOOL TRADITION

We believe Churches of Christ (and the Stone-Campbell Movement as a whole) have a vibrant spiritual heritage that invites us to participate in the emerging kingdom of God. Some have turned to Barton W. Stone for inspiration and others have noticed Alexander Campbell's spiritual fervor. It is a legacy that finds fulfillment neither in lifeless forms nor arrogant exclusivity. In this book, however, we turn our attention to the beginning of the twentieth century. One hundred years ago the Nashville (TN)-Bowling Green (KY) corridor was an epicenter of spiritual fervor. By 1906 David Lipscomb was living in Nashville, Tennessee, and James A. Harding was living in Bowling Green, Kentucky. They were both editors and college founders/teachers. They were the most highly respected leaders east of the Mississippi and south of the Ohio. They promoted an alternative tradition to what was dominant in Texas (i.e. *Firm Foundation* in Austin) at the time and to what was dominant in the Midwest (i.e., the Disciples of Christ). It was a "third way" in its own day. Just as Lipscomb and Harding battled the sectarianism they perceived in the *Firm Foundation* on their right, they also fought the accomodationism they perceived in the *Christian-Evangelist* (of St. Louis, which was on the trajectory of the contemporary Christian Church [Disciples of Christ]) and *Christian Standard* (of Cincinnati, which was on the trajectory of the contemporary Christian Church/Churches of Christ) on their left. While the former, in their view, created a sect, the latter accommodated itself, in their view, to American culture through deism, patriotism, and materialism.

Lipscomb and Harding, in contrast, promoted a kingdom vision that saw the world differently than either the right or left. Their influence was most strongly felt from 1891 to 1917. Lipscomb and Harding co-founded the Nashville Bible School (NBS) in 1891. Harding later founded Potter Bible College (PBC) at Bowling Green in 1901. Lipscomb edited the *Gospel Advocate* and Harding edited *The Way* (later

The Christian Leader and the Way). By 1917, Lipscomb had died and Harding was suffering from dementia (dying in 1922). But from 1891 to 1917 they successfully promoted the Christian life through teaching in their schools, writing in their papers, and conducting itinerant evangelistic meetings. We call their approach to the Way the "Nashville Bible School Tradition" (NBST).

This tradition advances a vibrant vision of the Christian life. God is dynamically introducing his kingdom into a fallen world. God graciously takes the initiative in relationships and actively cares for his people as he advances his kingdom through providence, miracle and the indwelling of the Holy Spirit. God opposes the Satanic kingdoms of the fallen world and objects to any allegiance to things in the world. This vision is God-centered and mission-oriented. It seeks the goal of God's fully consummated kingdom. It opposes patriotism, embraces a counter-cultural lifestyle, exalts the spiritual disciplines of prayer, Bible reading and caring for the poor, and values the weekly gathering of God's people around the table.

The Nashville Bible School Tradition contrasts with another tradition within Churches of Christ. In 1884 Austin McGary began publishing the *Firm Foundation* which opposed the "liberalism" of Lipscomb's *Advocate*. Generally, it embraced a sectarian understanding of baptism (i.e., only those immersed with the specific understanding that baptism was necessary for salvation are genuinely baptized), taught that the Holy Spirit only dwelled representatively in the believer through the word, embraced a deistic understanding of providence, and fully identified the church with the kingdom. We call this the "Texas Tradition."[2]

Though this Texas Tradition emerged in full view with the beginning of the *Firm Foundation*, it was promoted and developed by such luminaries as J. D. Tant and R. L. Whiteside. Indeed, Whiteside was often called the "David Lipscomb of Texas."[3] He epitomizes and perhaps is the person most responsible for the development of a consensus theology among Churches of Christ in the 1940-1950s.[4] Though graduating from the Nashville Bible School in 1898, he opposed their understanding of the kingdom. He led the fight against premillennialism (and its larger "apocalyptic" orientation), pacifism, and the personal indwelling of the Spirit. His theology saturated Churches of Christ through his commentary on Romans and his five-volume series *Sound Doctrine*, co-authored with C. R. Nichol.[5] Foy E. Wallace, Jr. illustrates his impact. No other "teacher" was more of a "mentor and model" to him than R. L. Whiteside.[6]

At the beginning of the twentieth century these two theological traditions dominated Churches of Christ, though there were other perspectives such as the Sommerites in the Midwest. These streams overlapped in many ways as they co-existed within Churches of Christ, but they were often at odds (as chapters in this book will demonstrate, though not every topic, of course, is a contrast). They held many beliefs in common—weekly Lord's Supper, immersion of believers for the remission of sins, high view of Scripture, plurality of elders, and *a cappella* music. In terms of ecclesiastical form, they appeared as one. However, the inner logic of their theological perspectives was fundamentally different. For example, while the Texas Tradition identified the church with the kingdom such that the church implemented the kingdom system that God inaugurated at Pentecost, the Nashville Bible School Tradition maintained that the kingdom was the dynamic work of God in the world that cannot be simply identified with the church. The significance of this difference, as well as other differences, between the two traditions will emerge in the course of the book.

Though the Nashville Bible School Tradition was prominent in the early years of the twentieth century, ultimately the Texas Tradition practically absorbed it in the south and became the majority perspective in the 1940s-1950s through the influence of such leaders as Whiteside and Wallace. However, we believe the Nashville Bible School Tradition is particularly compelling, more biblically authentic, and needed in the contemporary church. We hope not only to reacquaint the church with this spiritual heritage but to invite believers to participate in the kingdom life our spiritual ancestors envisioned. This book endeavors to facilitate the appropriation of communal practices, individual habits, and a kingdom vision that shaped the life and teachings of Lipscomb and Harding.

BIOGRAPHICAL BACKGROUND

David Lipscomb was born in Franklin County, Tennessee on January 21, 1831. He graduated from Franklin College in 1849 where he studied under Tolbert Fanning. Lipscomb was a close associate of Fanning when his mentor began the *Gospel Advocate* in 1855. Though the paper ceased publication during the Civil War, Lipscomb reissued the journal in 1866 and remained its editor till 1913 (dying in 1917). Through the *Gospel Advocate* Lipscomb wielded considerable influence in the South. In its pages, he appealed to the North to help poor southern churches, promoted a counter-cultural understanding of the church, protested the intrusion of the American Missionary Society into the South, contested the introduction of instrumental music in the churches, opposed the appearance of German liberal theology among the Disciples in the North, and combated what he regarded as the right-wing extremism of Austin McGary in Texas. In many ways, Lipscomb shaped the identity of Churches of Christ at the turn of the century as its most prominent editor.[7]

James A. Harding was born in Winchester, Kentucky on April 16, 1848. Graduating from Bethany College in 1869, he taught school in Hopkinsville (1869-1874) and Winchester (1875-1876, 1878-1879), Kentucky. Beginning in 1876, he became an itinerant evangelist, preaching protracted meetings from Canada to Florida and from New York to New Mexico. He conducted over three hundred protracted meetings ranging from ten days to seven weeks as he averaged ten sermons a week for seventeen years. For example, in 1883 he preached on three hundred days as he delivered over five hundred sermons. In addition, he conducted fifty debates, ten of them in 1888 alone.[8] In 1891 he moved to Nashville as founding president of NBS. Due to the presence of the school and intense evangelist work, the number of churches in Nashville grew from five in 1888 to fifty in 1910.[9] Harding continued his itinerant preaching during school breaks as well as editing

The Way (1899-1903) and *The Christian Leader and the Way* (1903-1912). To multiply efforts, Harding accepted the offer of the Potters to found a school in Bowling Green, Kentucky. In that first year (1901-1902), there were 100 students at NBS and 107 at PBC, whereas there were only 106 at NBS in 1900-1901. Due to failing health, he resigned the presidency in 1912, though he co-edited *The Christian Herald* and conducted evangelistic meetings until 1916. His periodic blackouts and dementia only permitted him intermittent activity until his death in Atlanta, Georgia (1922).[10]

David Lipscomb and James A. Harding were the most significant "Editor-Bishops" and educators ("Founder/President-Bishops") east of the Mississippi in the early twentieth century. Lipscomb is regarded

James A. Harding and David Lipscomb

as the "father" of southern Churches of Christ while Harding is the "father" of Bible Schools (Colleges) among Churches of Christ. Their students founded schools in Meaford (Ontario, Canada), Nova Scotia (Canada), Armenia (Persia), Valdosta (Georgia), Gunter (Texas), Bridgeport (Alabama), Odessa (Missouri), Tokyo (Japan), Cordell (Oklahoma), and Harper (Kansas) in the first two decades of the twentieth century. Their significance is partly demonstrated by the fact that two major educational institutions of the Churches of Christ are named Lipscomb University (Nashville) and Harding University (Searcy, Arkansas).

In addition to Lipscomb and Harding, two of their students are significant for exploring the Nashville Bible School Tradition. John Nelson Armstrong (1870-1944) attended NBS in 1893 where he married Harding's daughter. After graduation, he taught at NBS and then moved with Harding to teach at PBC. He ultimately became President of colleges at Odessa (Missouri), Cordell (Oklahoma), and Harper (Kansas). He served as President of Harding College from 1924 to 1936 and taught there until his death.[11]

Robert H. Boll (1875-1956) attended NBS from 1895 to 1900 where he taught German and French. After an itinerant ministry in Texas (1901-1903), he became minister for the Portland Avenue Church of Christ in Louisville, Kentucky, where he remained (except for one year in Lawrenceburg, Tennessee) for the rest of his life. While there he trained ministers in a Bible school which became Southeastern Christian College (located first in Louisville, then in Winchester, KY). He served as the front page editor of the *Gospel Advocate* from 1909-1915, but was dismissed due to his controversial millennial views. He then became and remained editor of the *Word and Work* until his death.[12]

Lipscomb, Harding, Armstrong and Boll, among others such as Standford Chambers, Flavil Hall, S. H. Hall, R. C. Bell, J. W. Shepherd, S. P. Pitman, William Webb Freeman, and E. H. Ijams, represent a trajectory in Churches of Christ that was vibrant and influential in the early part of the twentieth century, especially east of the Mississippi and south of the Ohio. Though we call this the Nashville Bible School Tradition, its influence was not limited to Nashville or the

R. H. Boll

mid-South. In fact, through the establishment of schools and the editorship of many papers, the Nashville Bible School Tradition had a national presence.

CONCLUSION

While we intend to focus on the positive dimensions of the NBST as we seek to reclaim some values for the present, we are also aware of its failings. Lipscomb and Harding were not perfect men. Indeed, we regret that they both embraced the 1906 division between the Churches of Christ and the Christian Church as a lamentable good, and Harding was a separatist as early as 1883.[13] They pursued an ecclesial hermeneutic ("command, example and inference") that we believe distorts more than it illuminates biblical theology. They often (just as we do) mirrored their own culture. Lipscomb, for example, believed the south was a kind of special preserve of righteousness where God was doing his best work. And they sometimes compromised their values in relation to their surrounding culture. Neither NBS nor PBC admitted African-

Americans (David Lipscomb College was pressured to correct this injustice in 1964) and they were both social segregationists in relation to race. Harding and Lipscomb sometimes failed to live out their own principles. They were not perfect, nor are we, though we are all accountable for how we live out the kingdom vision in our respective times.

Neither did Lipscomb and Harding agree on every point (nor did their students). PBC began because Harding opposed the incorporation and endowment of NBS.[14] They differed on some particulars about providence (Lipscomb was more oriented toward "order" in the universe while Harding was more focused on divine action), law and grace (Lipscomb stressed obedience to law in ways that are uncharacteristic of Harding), and the Holy Spirit (Lipscomb's understanding of the personal indwelling of the Spirit is ambiguous). The Nashville Bible School Tradition is not monolithic, but it is sufficiently coherent to form a theological trajectory.

Despite their failings and differences, Lipscomb and Harding sought transformation into the image of Christ. They yearned to participate in the kingdom of God on earth. Their spiritual vision, communal practices, and individual habits testify to their interest in spiritual formation. These are the values we seek to highlight, develop and apply to the church today. The spiritual practices of the Nashville Bible School Tradition are worth reclaiming and recovering as habits within the contemporary church. Their spiritual vitality challenges our contemporary faith and practice.

We will introduce that challenge to you and invite you—along with us—to respond by embracing life in the kingdom of God. The plan of each chapter is to devote the first part to reacquainting ourselves with the history and theology of the Nashville Bible School Tradition, while the second part will explore what we believe are the biblical and theological grounding of that spirituality for the present. The third part will seek to apply that biblical theology to the current practice of the church. Join us on this journey through the past into the present for the sake of the future.

PART I

KINGDOM DYNAMICS: DIVINE ACTION

Robert Clark Bell was a student at the NBS in the 1890s, later taught with Harding and Armstrong at PBC, and then with Armstrong at Western Bible and Literary College as well as at Cordell Christian College. He later became President of Thorp Springs Christian College, Dean of Harding College, and a teacher at Abilene Christian College.[1] Bell's 1951 autobiographical article stresses the impact Harding had on his life. Bell believed that the church needed revival by exposure to what has been called Harding's "apocalyptic" theology.[2] Bell thought the church needed an infusion of this transformational perspective in order "to save [it] from changing divine dynamics to human mechanics."[3]

Bell sensed a change among Churches of Christ in the mid-twentieth century. The church was "booming." New church buildings were springing up throughout the country and a new mission emphasis arose in the post-World War II era. Yet, Bell believed that the church had shifted theologically. It no longer, for the most part, valued its alien status. Patriotism and nationalism had swamped the church during World War II. The church had "moved across the tracks" and secured cultural respectability. It became socially comfortable and made peace with American cultural icons. Theologically, the church, for the most part, embraced a practical deism and denied the enabling personal presence of the indwelling Spirit. The "plan" of salvation focused on what humans do rather than on what God did or does. Church growth was a matter of executing the "plan" and building buildings. The church became saturated with human mechanics rather than divine dynamics.

This was a shift away from the theology of the NBST which focused on the dynamic nature of divine action in the world and in the lives of Christians. Their "apocalyptic" vision pointed toward God's active engagement with the world for the sake of his kingdom. God is no distant watchmaker but rather a king who rules his realm by entering it in order to effect his will. He is a loving Father who cares for his children even in the minutest details. He did not leave us with a Bible only to watch from his heavenly throne. On the contrary, God is present through the Holy Spirit who indwells his people as an active power that enables them to live faithfully in a fallen world.

Human mechanics cannot manipulate God and it cannot accomplish the ends of his kingdom. Only God can bring about his kingdom and therefore we pray "your kingdom come." The story of redemption does not continue by human design and power. Rather, the drama is performed in the present by divine power. God encounters humanity in their daily lives and by this dynamic presence transforms his people into his likeness. The power of the kingdom is not subject to human manipulation or institutional boundaries. It is the power of God present in the fallen world to transform it into a new creation.

TWO

SHADOWS OF THE SECOND COMING: "THY KINGDOM COME"

[T]he mission of his kingdom is to break in pieces and destroy all...kingdoms of human origin;...His kingdom shall not only break in pieces these kingdoms, but it shall consume them.[1]
—David Lipscomb (1889)

Christ came into this world to establish a kingdom which is antagonistic to all human authority, to all governments of the earth. Its mission is to break down and destroy them all.[2]
—James A. Harding (1903)

In the early twentieth century America was struggling with its newfound international significance. The United States had recently defeated Spain in the Spanish-American War (1898) and seized its own colonial empire that circled the globe. At the same time millions of poor, largely Catholic, immigrants braved the sea and the unknown for a new chance at life in the New World.

Protestant Christians viewed the rising stardom of America as the fulfillment of a divine destiny. They likewise believed the growing mass of Catholic "unbelievers" with alarm. What could be done to protect America's new importance in the world? What could preserve our liberty as Americans and Christians? Will these new Americans support our way of life? These questions could come from the four corners of America today.

N. P. Lawrence, an Indiana preacher, had the answer to these pressing concerns. It was not unique to him and no doubt had broad support within the Stone-Campbell Movement. He wrote to his friend James A. Harding that the secret to liberty and the survival of pure Christianity was supporting the government. Lawrence, for whom Harding expresses deep admiration,[3] wanted to elect Christians to positions of leadership in the government. He believed that if "the political liberty of this land" was to continue it would be by the "election of men who have shown fidelity to their country." He said "to place in offices of trust men who owe allegiance supremely to the Pope is to strike a blow at the heart of our liberty." Lawrence argued that having faithful Christians in government would lead to "a harvest of all that is desirable to a sanctified heart."

Harding's readers were nothing short of stunned by his reply to Lawrence. Far from being sanctified wisdom, Harding believed his friend espoused nothing short of treason. Lawrence had not betrayed his national heritage but rather his spiritual allegiance to the kingdom of God. Harding answered his friend with an article entitled "The Kingdom of Christ vs. The Kingdoms of Satan"[4] that exposed a core theological value of the NBST. Here the "apocalyptic" worldview bursts forth in all of its radical contours.[5]

Harding responded bluntly, "Christians are citizens of the kingdom of heaven, and their king is the Lord Jesus Christ; and as their king tersely puts it, 'No man can serve two masters.'" For Harding the civil government was not a necessary prop to help support the Christian faith but was actually a Satanic seduction away from utter dependence upon God.

A COUNTER-CULTURAL TRADITION

Harding's response to Lawrence ushers us into the self-understanding of the NBST which is articulated classically by David Lipscomb in *Civil Government*.[6] Harding, like Lipscomb, believed God created a pristine world. He formed humanity in his own image to live in his gracious presence. Indeed humanity was created in the image of God in order to share in the privilege of ruling as part of the divine family.[7] But the goodness of God's dominion was marred through human rebellion. Humanity freely surrendered the earth to Satan. In its war against the kingship of God, humanity set up rival "kingdoms," giving allegiance to them. But these kingdoms, including the United States of America, were inspired by the enemy of God.

With one foot in the primeval age and the other squarely in the shadows of the second coming, Harding believed that only God's government reigned from the first and only his will reign in the end. Viewing the mission of the messiah within the broad framework of the biblical narrative, Harding argued that Christ's fundamental purpose was to redeem God's creation by destroying the usurpers of God's kingdom. "Christ came to this earth," Harding writes, "that he might deliver the earth from Satan." God's battle with evil is a cosmic struggle that is fought in every dimension of God's creation.

The task of the messiah was broader than simply removing the guilt of sin. Rather the death struggle of the Suffering Servant was to defeat the powers that have corrupted creation and poisoned Adam's race. As Lipscomb put it,

> The object of God's dealing with man, and especially the mission of Christ to earth, was to rescue the world from the rule and dominion of the evil one, from the ruin into which it had fallen through sin, and to rehabilitate it with the dignity and the glory it had when it came from the hand of God.[8]

Christians have voluntarily enlisted in a mission to supplant all competitors to the kingdom of God. Satan's establishment of these alternative kingdoms was, in the words of R. H. Boll, the "crime of high treason."[9] Our task is to pray that God's will is done on earth as it is in heaven.

If the mission of Christ is to consume all human governments as competitors to the kingdom of God, then, Harding urged Lawrence, "let them run their own governments." The trouble, as Lipscomb saw it, was that many Christians have come to believe that human effort and government were "more essential to the world's well-being, than the Divine."[10] If Christians pursued the reign of God with half the vigor many follow politics and self-advancement, then there would be no need for civil government since there would be no rule on earth but God's. There would be no law but Christ's. There would be no courts but the churches of the Christ. "This is the ideal state for which every Christian should look, and for which he should work and pray."[11]

How then does a citizen of the kingdom of light relate to the governments that fill the earth? The same way Abraham related to the Canaanites. God's people have the same relation to prevailing government as the Hebrew slaves did to the Egyptians. Christians share the same values as the Israelite exiles in Babylon. The church's responsibility to any modern authority is the same as it was in the days of Rome. Harding characterized Christian existence in the world with the word "foreigner." Christians are resident aliens in a world that claims allegiance to the Prince of Darkness. We have the same responsibility that any sojourner would have. We obey all laws that do not conflict with our divine calling. We pay our taxes for the privilege of using the infrastructure. We also pray for leaders that we may lead peaceable lives. Since Scripture explicitly commands obedience, prayer and paying taxes, Christians submit to government in this way but they do not seek to advance the agenda of the kingdoms of this world.

To many contemporary Christians, Harding's view, shared by David Lipscomb, J. N. Armstrong and Robert H. Boll, borders on bizarre. Yet for the NBST it was the theological foundation for living with God. This tradition took seriously the biblical notion that Christians live in the shadows of the second coming—to live their lives as if God's will was being done on earth as it is in heaven. It lived in anticipation of the fullness of God's reign. The looming shadows of the reign of God fill the NBST with a powerful ethical vision.

The NBS founders believed that God's people were distinct people.

With roots deep in the soil of this eschatological vision, these founders did not define the kingdom of God primarily in institutional terms. For Lipscomb "the kingdom embraces the church, but it is," he writes, "more extensive in its signification. The kingdom of God embraces every thing and every person in the universe over which God rules as king."[12] Lipscomb clarifies the relation of the church and the kingdom by suggesting the kingdom goes through development until it reaches perfection.

> This kingdom now established will yet pass through successive stages of development until it ends in 'the everlasting kingdom of our Lord and Savior, Jesus Christ.' The kingdom in its present state is not called 'the everlasting kingdom,' but will grow into it. It is the same kingdom in a lower stage of growth and development.[13]

These leaders were not simply interested in being different from denominations. Being a distinct people is not primarily about worship styles, but nonconformity to secular values.[14] They understood the life of the kingdom as a call out of a pagan world into an entirely different way of life. A distinct people had values distinct from this age. Those living in the shadows of the second coming would view possessions from a radically different point of view. Christians live "lightly" in this present world. They are stewards of God's good gifts to be shared as freely as they were received. Relationships in the kingdom are shaped by what God desires. The poor are not considered a burden but are regarded as the preference of God's heart. The color of one's skin, in the shadow of the second coming, looses all relevance as a basis of relationship. Indeed, a church that is truly a beachhead of God's reign will risk cultural alienation for the sake of those victimized on the basis of social location and race.

However, according to Harding, the Father does not simply surrender his beloved creation to the Evil One. On the contrary, God is in history to redeem the fallen world. God has not surrendered the world to either the machinations of the god of this age nor to some system of laws in which he takes a hands off approach. God, through his Holy Spirit and his angels, is providentially spreading the leaven of grace and active in the affairs of this world.

The foundation of the NBST theological vision was this apocalyptic worldview. It was not fundamentally apolitical and anti-American, rather it was profoundly pro-kingdom. Christians had been transferred into a new reality. This counter-society voluntarily embraced a set of values, chiefly seen in the Sermon on the Mount, that are alien and absurd to the common sense of the fallen world. The church is God's city on a hill that cannot be hid, a light in the darkness for the redemption of the world. Christians are a new humanity that is put on display by God to draw everyone back to him.

Living in the shadows of the second coming meant that God was profoundly active in this world to redeem and restore it. God takes the initiative to repair the "vandalism of shalom" in creation.[15] As Boll notes, though Satan is the god of this age, the Creator is still the supreme sovereign. He dares to "interfere in the earth's affairs" and to guide it toward his gracious goal of restored fellowship with humanity.[16] This divine interference extends to individual lives as well. God calls us to a radical alien mentality, but he provides the power for such a life through his indwelling and empowering Holy Spirit that transforms us into image of his Son. Thus in this apocalyptic worldview, the kingdom reveals the extent of Christ's rule over us. Cruciform ethics and divine grace take center stage in God's outpost kingdom.

Harding, as did other members of this tradition, opposed speculating on dates about the return of Christ. But he notes "that for the last fifty or sixty years many godly men have believed that the time of his coming is near."[17] Christians should discern the times and signs while they live in anticipation of that glorious day. Grasping the significance of this foundation is important for understanding why this tradition was dedicated to peace and opposed bloodshed in the name of nationalism, why it chose a counter-cultural refugee lifestyle as opposed to feeling at home in this world, and why the Sermon on the Mount was so important for them. In short if we understand this orientation we will understand both why and how they were "distinct" people.

RESIDENT ALIENS IN THE BIBLICAL STORY

The apocalyptic worldview enables us to discern the major contours of the biblical drama. Like a powerful searchlight in the darkness, as Lipscomb observed, it highlights the "key notes" of the biblical story.[18] The true beauty of living in the shadow of the second coming, Hughes argues, is that it forces us to grasp the major themes of scripture rather than its minor or obscure details.[19]

When we step back to watch the flow of biblical history, it becomes evident that Lipscomb and Harding did indeed grasp, in a profound way, a key motif of Scripture. The Lord created the world in love (cf. Ps 136) and established a paradise of *shalom*. The first chapters of Genesis testify to the world as it was meant to be, a place filled with harmony between humanity and the world, a place where men and women equally imaged God, and a place where the gracious presence of God was experienced. There was *shalom* between God, humanity and the cosmos. But Genesis 3 tells us the world that was is not the world that is. The goodness of creation was polluted through rebellion. Sin, the disease with a thousand faces, now dominates this once pristine world.

This insurrection brought alienation from the divine presence and the disintegration of relations within the human community. This present age is characterized by death, anguish, lust and violence. But God purposed to restore creation to its original blessedness, to restore *shalom* upon the earth. The prophets had Spirit-inspired visions of that day.

> Then justice will dwell in the wilderness,
> and righteousness abides in the fruitful field.
> The effect of righteousness will be peace,
> and the result of righteousness, quietness and trust forever.
> My people will abide in a peaceful habitation,
> in secure dwellings, and in quiet resting places. (Isa 32:16-18)

Amos had visions of Chardonnay dripping from the trees and flowing like rivers (Amos 9:13-15). Micah envisioned a time when hostilities would cease and weapons would be turned into farming implements (Micah 4.1-5; cf. Isa 2:1-5). These prophetic portraits testify to a longing for the return to the way things ought to be—for a time when God would once again reign, when justice and peace are the norm, when *shalom* would be restored.

To accomplish this goal, God called an ever-growing minority to be his representatives of the way life ought to be. This community, shaped by shadows of the coming reign of God, is a light in the darkness, revealing the heart of God to a world searching for life and hope.

Often, in both Testaments, God's people are pictured as a struggling band of nomads and refugees. God's people in the Old Testament were aliens in hostile territory. God chose Abraham out of love (Deut 7:7-9) to embark upon a journey to a destination he did not know. Though living in a land that would one day belong to his people, the friend of God was always a stranger in Canaan. Israel found herself sojourning as an alien for hundreds of years in a land that eventually enslaved her. Throughout her history, even in her own land, Israel was harried on all sides. Israel was an outsider in a pagan world. Israel, as the manifestation of God's kingdom, was to display the "splendor" of the Lord (Isa 49:3). But instead of leading nations into the embrace of Yahweh, Israel mimicked pagan values. Thus Ezekiel laments that God's own people led the nations to blaspheme the name of God (Ezek 36. 16ff). God, however, refused to give up on his people and proposed to wash them, create a new heart in them, and place his Spirit in them so they can truly live as his people (Ezek 36:25-27).

Just as Israel was a colony in the world, so the church likewise is an alien subculture in an age hostile to God. Yet, the power of conformity did not die with the saints of the Old Testament. Its specter faces Christians of every generation and nationality. We too become acclimated to our ethnic and cultural surroundings. It is not only the Israelites of Samuel's day that wished to be like the nations around them. We become comfortable with the world's politics. We become enamored with the power of mammon. We imbibe the world's racial prejudices. Yet like Abraham in his tent and the Israelites in the Nile Delta, we understand that we are not at home. We groan with creation itself for the revelation of a home in the new heaven and new earth. "But in keeping with his promise we are looking forward to a new heaven and a new earth, the home of the righteous" (2 Pet 3:13; cf. Rom 8:18-25).

The author of Hebrews highlights this pilgrim imagery in the heart of his famous catalogue of heroes as if it were essential to biblical faith.

> All these people were still living by faith when they died. They did not receive the things promised; they only saw them and welcomed them from a distance. And they admitted that they were aliens and strangers on earth. People who say such things show that they are looking for a country of their own.... Instead they were longing for a better country—a heavenly one. Therefore God is not ashamed to be called their God, for he has prepared a city for them. (Heb 11:13-16)

The author does not appeal to this pilgrim story for mere historical reasons but because his readers are themselves sojourners.[20] They are welcome neither in the Jewish synagogue nor in the Roman gymnasium. As sojourners in their culture they were truly living something that seems inherent to the biblical drama. The life of faith, life in the kingdom, is a life lived in the shadows of the second coming. To live in the shadows is to live in anticipation of God's ultimate victory. It is characterized by supreme hope in the reality of God's kingdom. We live our lives in the present age knowing things are not as they should be but with the expectation of what they will be. Biblical faith is lived as if the "heavenly" city has been planted on earth. We live as if the future is already present.

The "alien" status of the church is pervasive in the New Testament. Paul declares "our citizenship is in heaven" (Phil 3:20). James Moffatt vividly captured the original: "we are a colony of heaven." A colony is a beachhead on alien soil. It is surrounded by foreign country, strange language and perverse life-styles and values. Paul saw his converts as strangers in a strange land who bore witness to the Lordship of the coming Christ through transformed lives.

Peter joins this chorus of voices. He addresses his first letter to God's elect whom he describes as "aliens" or "refugees" (TEV) in the world. Some, it seems, are tempted to make peace with the pagan culture by assimilating into it. They are in danger of losing their distinctiveness. Thus Peter writes:

> Beloved, I urge you, as aliens and exiles, to abstain from the desires of the flesh, that wage war against the soul. Conduct yourselves honorably among the Gentiles, so that, though they malign you as evildoers, they may see your honorable deeds and glorify God when he comes to judge. (1 Pet 2:11-12)

Peter's appeal is radical. Disciples are not distinct from other believers. Rather they are different from this age. But their distinctiveness is not some kind of elitism. Rather, as free people (1 Pet 2:16), Christians are priests engaged in ministry on behalf of the world that rejects them. Justin Martyr, a mid-second century pagan turned disciple, testifies to the journey early Christians made in their value systems:

> We who formerly rejoiced in uncleanness of life and now embrace chastity; we who also used magical arts and have now dedicated ourselves to the good and unbegotten God; we who valued above all things the acquisition of wealth and possessions, now we bring what we have into a common stock and give to every one who is in need; we who hated one another and killed one another and would not eat with those of another race and now since the manifestation of Christ have a common life and pray for our enemies and try to win over those who hate us without just cause.[21]

To live in the shadow of the second coming is to take seriously the ethic of Jesus. The peculiarity of disciples is not that they wear quaint clothing or don't use modern technology. Rather their strangeness is located in their embrace of an ethic the world considers nonsense. The church is a place where humanity honors its promises, loves its enemies, tells the truth, embraces the poor, and suffers for righteousness.[22] These community traits are the essence of Jesus' Sermon on the Mount. It is a community where God's will is done on earth as in heaven.

Lipscomb was dismayed by the general rejection of the principles of this sermon as binding on Christians. Even in Churches of Christ some, due to their dispensational hermeneutic (where everything before Pentecost and since Moses was part of the old covenant), believed the Gospels and Acts 1 belonged to the old covenant. J. C. Holloway, editor of *Defender of the Word*, for example, wrote that the sermon was only given to the apostles for a special mission and modern Christians follow a more reasonable ethic.[23] But for Lipscomb the discourse contains "the living and essential principles of the religion the Savior came to establish, those which must pervade and control the hearts…of men, without which no man can be a Christian."[24]

The biblical story begins with some wandering Arameans and closes with a challenge to choose between two cities, Babylon or the New Jerusalem.[25] In between prophets, apostles and the Savior himself call the redeemed to view themselves as resident aliens looking for the consummation of the kingdom. The church functions as God's demonstration of what the world would look like if his *shalom* was restored to his good creation; what the world would look like if the divine will was done on earth as it is in heaven.

BECOMING SOJOURNERS

Living as an alien has never been an easy journey. Humans have an innate desire to accommodate and assimilate into their peer group. Sojourners are victimized. Migrants are frequently underpaid and with no recourse to justice. Temporary residents are, at times, abused. Refugees are habitually disenfranchised by the ruling powers. Living in tents quickly looses its rustic appeal for those in awe of the world's glamour. An ancient Jewish sage can speak for all of us when he confesses the frustration of outsiders.

> It is a miserable life to go from house to house;
> as a guest you should not open your mouth;
> You will play the host and provide drink without being thanked,
> and besides this you will hear rude words like these:
> 'Come here, stranger, prepare the table;
> let me eat what you have there.'
> 'Be off, stranger, for an honored guest is here;
> my brother has come for a visit,
> and I need the guest-room.'
> It is hard for a sensible person to bear
> scolding about lodging and the
> insults of the moneylender." (Sirach 29:24-28)

Despite its difficulty early Christians retained a sense of alienation from the world for some time after the apostles. They viewed the Roman games and temples through the shadows and found them wanting. Christians prayed for the Emperor and obeyed his laws but refused to serve in his armies.[26] They shared their possessions with the poor and took in the abandoned. In their communities race seemed to disappear as matters of consequence. In the second century an anonymous Christian tried to explain to Diognetus, a non-believer, how Christians viewed the world. In words that border on eloquent, a picture of the resident alien is painted for the readers of this early Christian apology.

> While they [Christians] dwell in cities of Greeks and barbarians as the lot of each is cast, and follow the native customs in dress and food and other arrangements of life, yet the constitution of their own citizenship, which they set forth, is marvelous, and confessedly contradicts expectation. They dwell in their own countries but only as sojourners; they bear their share in all things as citizens and they endure all hardships as

> strangers. Every foreign country is a fatherland to them, and every fatherland is foreign....Their existence is on Earth, but their citizenship is in heaven. They obey the established laws, and they surpass the laws in their own lives. They love all men, and they are persecuted by all.[27]

Ironically, Christians are the best of all citizens for they are citizens of the world. They love all as family. Perhaps it is because they do "love all" and refuse to bring evil to another that they are "persecuted by all." With the long shadows of the second coming falling, Christians are enemies and partisans of none.[28]

Through the years, however, this kingdom vision was lost through the institutionalization of the church. Church, here, does not mean the people who have been called out of this present age by grace into covenant with God. Rather "church" became concern for proper doctrine, and rather esoteric doctrine couched in Greek philosophy. "Church" became involved in power struggles within itself and in time even secular government became enmeshed in what was once a small band of rag-tag believers in a Messiah who was killed by that very government. When this happened Christianity became Christendom. Christendom was the epitome of the cultural church, that is, Christianity without the demands of the cross. Every one is a Christian but few are disciples of Jesus.

At various times and places numerous groups protested the cultural church.[29] Monasticism itself was a revolt against its growing worldliness. Ironically many of these followers were branded heretics and brutalized by the now powerful institutional church. One such group, the Anabaptists, was greatly admired by Lipscomb.[30] The Anabaptists challenged both Roman Catholic and Protestant establishments. In essence they said that Christians are made, not born. They recaptured the distinctiveness of living in the shadow of another age. Baptism became, once again, a voluntary mark of discipleship. To be baptized meant considering the cost of walking along the way of the cross behind the Lord Jesus. Baptism was nothing less than a declaration of allegiance to God's transcendent kingdom and a rejection of this present age. One was not a Christian because she assented to a few incomprehensible doctrinal propositions. Rather, Christians choose a life that is fundamentally reoriented toward God's kingdom. Anabaptists sought nothing less than the restoration of the resident alien life that is so embedded in the biblical narrative. Lipscomb understood this. Using the imagery of "separation," he believed that the church can never claim to be restored until it has reclaimed its alien status.

> If the church ever attains to its primitive purity and efficiency it must be by a return to this clearly established principle of the separation of all its members from worldly governments, and the consecration of the affections, time, means and talents of all its members to the up building of the church of God and the salvation of the world.[31]

To live life in the shadows of the second coming often means taking unpopular stances, even with fellow Christians. This worldview, as with the Anabaptists, forces us to take the radical nature of baptism seriously. Baptism is profoundly ethical in nature (Rom 6; Col 2:12-14). God uses this moment to crucify our old nature and resurrect us to a new life. This new life entails seeing the world itself from the perspective of the new creation.[32] Baptism entails the inauguration of a new humanity, one that is no longer defined by race, gender, nationality or political orientation (Gal 3:27-28). This means we are no longer defined by ideologies important to the present age. To put it another way, baptism explains why disciples do not make the best Americans, Germans or Ethiopians.[33] This apocalyptic orientation claims that we have more in common with a rural disciple of Jesus in Pakistan, who has never traveled a mile from her home than with my neighbor across the street living in middle class America. While appreciative of our American heritage, we affirm we are strangers and aliens even in this land.

CONCLUSION

To live in the shadows of the second coming means living lightly as we resist the temptations of materialism. We live by the good graces of our Lord and share those gifts willingly and sacrificially. We stand not only as God's witness to the kingdom but we are agents of reconciliation and redemption in the world. Like leaven in the lump we permeate divine justice in a world that operates by the law of greed. As the salt of the earth we are cast into a world dominated by pollution to preserve a divine witness.

To live in the shadows of the second coming means we believe that there is more power in the prayers of sisters in their golden years than any decision made by the President, Congress or the United Nations. Scripture challenges us to live in exclusive allegiance to Jesus Christ. The call is daring but refreshing.

DISCUSSION QUESTIONS

1. What do you find compelling about worldview of the NBST? How might this challenge the contemporary church? What do you think Harding or Lipscomb might say about us today?

2. Do you believe that God has called the contemporary church to a refugee life? What are the values of a resident alien? Why is it difficult to conceive of ourselves as resident aliens?

3. Do you tend to get more emotional about politics or God's kingdom?

4. Do you think that Jesus held "political" views? If he did what might those views be?

CHALLENGES

Develop a pattern of regular meditation on the Sermon on the Mount to shape your worldview according to the ethic of Jesus.

Cross a racial or cultural barrier this week for the sake of the kingdom: attend a Spanish speaking church service; invite a person of a different race for a meal at your home.

PRAYER

Abba, Father, we humbly, but gratefully, come before you seeking your Spirit inspired power for our lives. Humbly because we freely admit we partake in the fallen structures of this evil age. Gratefully because we cling to the grace so bountifully give for Christ's sake. We beseech you to complete the process begun in our baptism that we become one with your kingdom agenda. Make your church truly a city on a hill that cannot be hid. Hear our prayer, Amen.

SUGGESTED RESOURCES

Craig G. Bartholomew and Michael W. Goheen, *The Drama of Scripture: Finding Our Place in the Biblical Story* (Grand Rapids: Baker Academic, 2004)

Lee Camp, *Mere Discipleship: Radical Christianity in A Rebellious World* (Grand Rapids: Brazos, 2003)

Ronald J. Sider, *The Scandal of the Evangelical Conscience: Why Are Christians Living Just Like the Rest of the World?* (Grand Rapids: Baker, 2005)

John Howard Yoder, *The Politics of Jesus* (Grand Rapids: Eerdmans, 1972)

Benjamin J. Walsh and Sylvia C. Keesmaat, *Colossians Remixed: Subverting the Empire* (Downers Grove, IL: InterVarsity, 2004)

THREE

GOD STILL WORKS: TRUSTING GOD'S PROVIDENCE

We should pray to God to give us whatever is best for us,
wealth or poverty, honor or humiliation, health or sickness, life or death;
being sure that whatever he gives to his dutiful child will be a blessing;
resting in the faith that for all that we sacrifice or suffer for him
we may expect a hundredfold reward, even in this present time.
—James A. Harding (1902)[1]

All the events connected with our lives are more completely under his guidance and direction, and are more fully controlled and overruled by him than were those of any other people in the world…The failure to recognize God's hand in the events that befall us, causes us to complain, whine, repine over the misfortunes—as we consider them—of life, and to indulge in bitter, wicked, envious thoughts toward others, and to live in anxiety and dread as to the present and the future.
—David Lipscomb (1869)[2]

David Lipscomb married Margaret Zellner on July 23, 1862 in Maury County, Tennessee, south of Nashville. It was a dangerous time. Fifty thousand Union troops occupied Nashville. The wedding gift from Margaret's mother was the last available set of knives and forks in Columbia. Food was scarce; a pound of coffee cost five hundred Confederate dollars. After teaching for a year close to the

Alabama/Tennessee border, the couple moved near Nashville to Lipscomb's farm on the other side of the Confederate-Union line.

Zellner Lipscomb was born amidst such uncertainty but lived only nine months.[3] His father and mother crossed the North/South line to bury him in Maury County. It was a devastating blow. The Lipscombs never had any other children, though they raised several of their relative's offspring. Lipscomb had "hoped to raise [Zellner] up to work for the Lord," he once remarked to T. B. Larimore, and now he would "have to work all the harder."[4] The hurt ran deep and even thirty years later Lipscomb was known to display public grief at the thought of Zellner's death.

The environs around Nashville suffered tremendous loss in 1864-1865 and the Lipscombs shared in this misery. Two of his cousins were killed in the fighting of 1864. Poverty and hunger overwhelmed the region; farms were destitute of even their animals.[5] The Lipscombs lost two-thirds of everything they owned and lived on the edge of starvation.[6] These conditions continued, though with steady improvement, in the middle Tennessee region for a decade after the war.

The Lipscombs were acquainted with grief and no strangers to the crucible of suffering. And neither was James A. Harding. He married Carrie M. Knight on October 4, 1871, but two of his three children with Carrie died before their first birthday.[7] After only five years of marriage, Carrie passed away. Marrying Pattie Cobb on March 27, 1878, Harding fathered six more children but outlived three of them.[8] In all, Harding outlived five of his nine children as well as his first wife.[9]

The quotes that head this chapter may seem rather naïve to those unacquainted with their stories. These couples knew suffering in ways beyond what most experience in our contemporary churches. And yet they persevered in faith, and more than that, saw the hand of God in their lives, even in their suffering.

Lipscomb, for example, discerned a divine purpose in the Civil War similar to that expressed by Lincoln in his Second Inaugural Address. "Since the end of the war," Lipscomb wrote, "we have never had a doubt but that it was the purpose of the great Father of the universe to destroy slavery."[10] That the Northern army was God's battle-axe, Lipscomb wrote, "we have no doubt." But the North was no righteous avenger. The North, Lipscomb prophesied, would also experience its divine judgment. "It is folly and deception for a people," he wrote, "to think that because they are used to punish other nations and are successful in war, therefore they are better or more favored of God than the nations they conquer. The wicked are the sword of the Lord."[11]

Harding also reflected on his suffering in terms of divine purpose. Sears reports that "Carrie's death, painful as it was to bear, Harding felt later was a blessing for both her and for him. With her feeble health he could never have accomplished the great work he was destined to do."[12] Everything that happens, according to Harding, serves God's purposes. "He loves us and he allows no pain, no sorrow, no disappointment to come to us except it be for our own good." Despite losing two children and a wife to death before his twenty-sixth birthday, he could still advise a fellow-sufferer to pray "as God wills" because "God knows best."[13]

What underlies such strong confidence and trust in God's working is a high view of providence, especially what was called "special providence."

SPECIAL PROVIDENCE

In the late nineteenth and early twentieth century, the Disciples witnessed the emergence of a deistic understanding of God's relationship to the world within their ranks.[14] According to this view, God regulates the world through natural law and is not personally involved in the course of history. Some denied any kind of special providence at all other than ancient miracles,[15] while others limited special providence only to spiritual ends in relation to the soul and the gospel.[16] The former believe God established the natural order and does not involve himself in the world, while the latter believes God is only involved in providing inner strength and comfort. Others, like Lipscomb and Harding, clung to belief in meticulous (detailed) special providence.[17] Many parts of the Stone-Campbell Movement developed a modified

Deism according to which God had intervened in the past with miracles, but now works only through the mediation of the created order's natural laws and through the words of Scripture.

For Lipscomb that emerging Deism was "rationalism" and "practical infidelity."[18] For Harding it reduced God to a "silent partner." Anything less than God's active involvement, according to Harding, is "unbelief" and "more injurious to the Church" than any other lie Satan ever circulated.[19] "Is it possible," Harding asked, "that the divine members of this great partnership have ceased to have anything whatever to do with its affairs, so far as this earth is concerned?"[20] Both Lipscomb and Harding answered with a resounding "No!" Instead, God is active in every aspect of his world for his own purposes and for the sake of his people.

In particular, they both saw special providence in a fallen world as disciplinary, pedagogical, probationary, and preparatory for better things to come. God intends to restore his creation to its original status where human beings serve as co-regents with God over his world. Consequently, God will allow "no purpose of his to be thwarted" as he prepares them to reign with him in the future. Humanity, according to Harding, was "created to reign for ever and ever"—first in the original creation, but given the fall, now to reign with Christ in the millennium and then with the Father in the new heaven and new earth.[21] Faithful service prepares humanity for their future role as co-regents in God's new creation.

Given the tragic detour into fallenness that human beings have taken creation, God uses the circumstances of life to train humanity for the future. Blessing and suffering alike are tools in divine hands to disciple, teach, test and prepare humanity for their future role. Consequently, human beings live in this present fallen world as a moment of trial or probation. "This is a life of preparation, of probation, of trial or choice," Lipscomb wrote, "in which we make our choice, undergo our schooling, develop the character that will decide our destiny and work out our fate in the world to come."[22] God "prove[s] and test[s]" humanity to "see who is worthy to stand in his everlasting kingdom."[23] By this means God conforms us to his image, and he uses all the divine resources for that goal. "We are thus gradually trained through successive stages," according to Lipscomb, "and molded in character into the likeness of God, and so fitted to stand beside his Son, to bear his likeness."[24]

God's overruling providence, then, directs all things to the end that God desires. Intimately involved in the life of every human being, God is at work to draw people to himself and usher in his kingdom. Specifically, God makes special provision for those who love and trust him. Like a trainer preparing an athlete for his contest, God attends to the needs of his people. "God will give [his saint] wisdom, guidance, strength, protection and any and everything else, material and spiritual, that he needs for his welfare here."[25]

This stands in contrast to those like L. S. White of Dallas, Texas, who believed that God only works through natural laws and is bound by the order within his universe. Harding confronted this position head-on in a discussion with White through the pages of the *The Christian Leader and the Way*.[26] The "debate" was a classic clash between one tradition which trusted that in the past God provided the order that humanity now worked and the tradition that trusted in God's active providing. While Harding was criticized for his "trust theory," Harding preferred to call it "*faith practice*." People of faith live with the confidence that God is faithful in both prosperity and adversity, and they may trust him at all times.

The discussion revealed two fundamentally different conceptions of God. For White God is the provider of the "system"—the natural order. Our task is to work the system. For Harding, in sharp contrast, God is a "father" who loves and nurtures his children. Harding grounds the relationship between God and his creatures in the relational metaphor of "father" and "children."

> I believe that God loves his faithful children with a very great love. I believe he is very near to them, takes great pleasure in them, knows their needs perfectly, and that he can sup-

> ply their wants at any time, anywhere, under any circumstances. Indeed, I believe he loves these faithful children so much he guards them with a perfect care. So great is this love, so perfect the care, there is nothing can befall anyone of them—whether it comes from heaven, earth or hell, from God, angel or devil—that does not bring a blessing.[27]

While White thinks in terms of a deistic system where we work for our food and depend on our own "business," Harding trusts in the Father's gift of "daily bread." White's conception of God is rather impersonal and his relationship with humanity mostly legal. Harding thinks in more relational terms as a father intimately involved in providing, caring and attending to the needs of his children.

For Harding, unlike White, God is not bound by anything but his promise. Even "natural law" is a human construct rather than a boundary for God. Natural law is merely our human apprehension of the normal ways in which God works, but God's acts "continually [bring] about results by means of natural laws in ways that are incomprehensible to us."[28] These acts are divine miracles—it is "something that God does," but the "*how*" is "beyond human comprehension."[29] While God in the past authenticated his messengers with miracles, "far oftener has he performed them," Harding believed, "in protecting and blessing and guiding his children." And this God continues to do. God is constantly "in some way incomprehensible to mortal men…causing all things to work together for their good."[30] The people of God need miracles as much today as they did in the apostolic age. Angels of mercy, for example, fill the earth to perform miracles on behalf of the children of God.[31] Thus, God does "as much for his children as he ever did."[32] In contrast to those who think "that all divine interventions have ceased since the death of the apostles" such that "God gave the word and stopped," Harding believed that God is actively working within his cosmos for the sake of his people.[33]

Three texts were particularly important to Harding. These texts, along with "thousands" of others, should rid the Christian of all "anxiety."[34] Psalm 37 was for Harding "one of the most delightful passages in the Word of God." In particular, he drew strength from Psalm 37:5, "Trust in the LORD and do good" (KJV). God is faithful and he will grant success to whoever follows that "plan."[35] Indeed, this was Harding's own financial plan for preaching the gospel. Some called it his "trust theory" but for Harding it was his confidence that God would care for his every need, including "temporal blessings" like the promise of food and clothing.[36]

Matthew 6:33 was Harding's clarion call for everyone to devote themselves to the interests of the kingdom without any anxiety about food and clothing. This promise functions as a kind of "contract" between God and his people.[37] It applies to whomever operates "his business, whatever that may be, solely for the advancement of God's kingdom." Christians should regard themselves, even in their vocations and careers, as "being in the world simply and solely" for sake of the kingdom.[38] In practical application, Harding never stipulated an amount for preaching, never incurred indebtedness, never saved any significant amount of money but gave it away (he claims he never had more than fifty dollars in his possession at any particular time and never had any possessions that ever totaled more than five hundred dollars), and went wherever the Lord led him.[39] In this Harding consciously imitated the practices of the Stoneite preacher Samuel Rogers which he had learned from reading his autobiography.[40]

Harding probably quoted Romans 8:28 more than any other text. No matter what the circumstances, God is at work for the good of his children—even in the midst of trouble. "If God is with him," he wrote, "though he may have poverty, persecution, hatred, imprisonment and contempt, he may confidently believe that all of these are blessings, and that sooner or later he will plainly see that they are, and will greatly rejoice in them." Even what believers suffer function as blessing because God rules over its purpose. "There is no exception to this rule [Romans 8:28]; it is as eternal and unchangeable as God himself."[41]

GOD RULETH O'ER EVERYTHING

One of the more significant threads running throughout Scripture is the affirmation that the Lord reigns (Pss. 93:1; 96:10; 97:1; 98:6; 99:1). Whether it is Joseph in prison, or David chased by Saul, or Jeremiah in the pit, or Jesus on the cross, or Peter in prison, or martyred saints in Asia Minor, believers have affirmed—whether in lament or praise—the sovereignty of God over his world. Whether we experience prosperity or adversity (cf. Ecc 7:13-14), God still sits on his throne and nothing escapes his attention or care.

Even in lament, believers have still trusted in God's royal care. For example, Psalm 10 begins by questioning God: "Why, O LORD, do you stand far off? Why do you hide yourself in times of trouble?" (10:1). The wicked oppress the weak and poor. The arrogant boast in their prosperity. They create trouble and believe that God does not notice their evil (10:2-11). But the psalmist demands God do something. "Arise, LORD! Lift up your hand, O God. Do not forget the helpless" (10:12). This petition is rooted in two anchors: God cares and God reigns. God knows the afflictions of his people and he will act on their behalf. The psalmist prays, "But you, O God, do see trouble and grief; you consider it to take it in hand" (10:14). God hears the prayers of his people and he will respond to their afflictions (10:17-18). God is able because he is the sovereign King. "The LORD is King for ever and ever" (10:16). God can break the arm of the wicked because he is the sovereign Lord.

This sovereign Lord is, therefore, no malicious tyrant, but a loving Father who cares about his people. Consequently, we trust that he has the best interests of his people in mind. God has a purpose for the trials and troubles his people experience. God cares and God is sovereign. Nothing on his part, then, is malicious and nothing is arbitrary. The Lord is praised for his "love and faithfulness" and also for his sovereignty, "Our God is in heaven, he does whatever pleases him" (Ps 115:1, 3; cf. Ps 135:6). God blesses his people out of his love and secures those blessings by his sovereignty.

God is active in the world for the sake of his people. He has a goal and everything that happens serves that goal. That goal is not necessarily our physical comfort, but our spiritual fellowship with him. God is more interested in our holy communion with him than whether we are healthy or wealthy. God is more interested in our faith than our transitory pleasure. Whether or not God permits or causes any particular event in the world, it is enough to say that God is sovereign over all events, and that nothing happens without his permission. God has a reason for his permission or his actions. He wants a people to share his fellowship and serve as his royal representatives upon the earth. God, then, permits or causes whatever happens for the sake of this original intent.

We are designed for happiness, but we have always looked for it in the wrong places. We seek the creature rather than the Creator. We seek sensual pleasure rather than communion with God. We choose the tangible over the intangible, the seen over the unseen, and the temporal over the eternal. We choose ourselves, others or things over God. We have been looking for love in all the wrong places. We promote, use and even distort whatever we possess (power, wealth, fame, knowledge, talents, family, even religion) in the hope that we might find happiness in those things. We are restless until we are happy, and we are unhappy because we are restless. God's goal for us is happiness, but it is not the kind of happiness which we self-absorbed, fallen humans seek. We seek our own selves, autonomy, and independence. God's goal, however, is that we find happiness in relationship with him. Happiness is to enjoy God forever.

God uses troubles, tribulations and trials to generate, strengthen or refine our faith. God is interested in our faith as a means of communion with him. As a result, he will use whatever means necessary to turn us from unbelief to belief, from distrust to trust; to turn us from the sensual pleasures of self-interestedness to the joy of relationship with him. God will use the circumstances of this fallen world to accomplish his eternal goal, and this involves the discipline, training and testing of his people.

No matter what our present experience—whether hardship or

joy—"we know that in all things God works for the good of those who love him" (Romans 8:28).This has been a favorite text for many sufferers throughout the centuries. It assures us of God's active involvement ("works"), his comprehensive care ("all things"), his benevolent purpose ("for good"), and his relational intent ("those who love him"). The comprehensive care includes the suffering that is Paul's topic in Romans 8:18-27. This relationality is expressed through the indwelling Spirit who prays for us with words we cannot express (Rom 8:26-27). His active involvement includes the gift of "all things" (Rom 8:33). His benevolent purpose, though often (if not always) unclear in our particular sufferings, is focused on his goal—to conform us to the image of Christ (Rom 8:29). Romans 8:28 testifies to God's special providence.

LIVING BY FAITH

Trust is the key word. Our response to God's sovereignty is faith rather than pride; dependence rather than self-reliance. This child-like trust does not understand everything. Quite the contrary, faith seeks understanding rather than understanding grounding faith. We live by faith, not by sight.

Consequently, the journey of faith is a process. Our experiences draw us deeper into depths of faith as we encounter life's hills and valleys. The more we understand, the more life's enigmas manifest themselves. The more we understand, the greater our need to trust. The more we understand, the more we know we don't know. We live by faith, not by sight.

Reason to Trust

The journey of faith is filled with questions, doubt and hardship. Trust is not facile. It is learned through the school of hard-knocks. The Psalmists lament and question, complain and petition. Though trusting in their Shepherd, they wonder where the Shepherd is when the sheep are being slaughtered (Ps 44:22). Their faith questions, "Has his unfailing love vanished forever?" (Ps 77:8). "O Lord, where is your former great love?" (Ps 89:49). Even Jesus questioned, "My God, My God, why have you forsaken me?" (Mt 27:46 quoting Ps 22:1).

But believers have reason to trust, even when it seems like God has abandoned us and his world. There is ground for the confidence of faith even while faith questions and sometimes wavers. The root of our trust—the place where we see the depth of God's interest in us—is found in Jesus, the revelation of the Father's love in the power of the Spirit.

Jesus demonstrates the loving care of God. The one who was rich became poor for our sakes (2 Cor 8:9). The one who existed in the form of God humiliated himself to take on the form of a servant (Phil 2:5-8). In his humiliation and poverty, Jesus ministered compassionately to the poor, demonized and sick. Preaching the good news of the kingdom, he demonstrated the caring love of God by healing every kind of brokenness (Mt 9:36-37). Jesus reveals the compassionate Father. He humbled himself even to the suffering of the cross. Hanging on the cross, he loved us and announced the love of God (John 3:16).

Jesus demonstrates the sovereign power of God. His ministry was a triumph over the brokenness of the world. He announced the good news of the kingdom by healing the sick and raising the dead. He triumphed over Satan's cohorts and defeated Satan through obedience to the Father. And, climactically, though death enveloped him, he conquered it through resurrection. The sovereign reign of the kingdom God broke into the world in the person of Jesus and announced the coming reality of the eternal kingdom. God will reign in all the earth, and even death will not thwart God's purposes.

Because of Jesus we trust even when we live in circumstances that call into question that trust. Jesus reveals that God loves us, cares for us, and rules his world for our sake.

Trusting God

Trust is supported by two pillars. One is the transcendent sovereignty of God over his world and the other is God's immanent loving care for his people. When the Psalmist experienced the betrayal of friends and was endangered by assaults on his position in the community, he took refuge in God as his fortress and rock (Ps 62). "Trust in him at all times," the Psalmist encourages Israel. "Pour out your hearts to him for God is our refuge." His confidence is rooted in two things he has heard about God—two aspects of God he knows from the stories of Israel: "you, O God, are strong, and that you, O Lord, are loving."

Israel learned to trust God through its history with him. God has a track record that grounds our trust. In his compassion, God heard the cries of his people in Egypt and sovereignly liberated them from Egyptian slavery. God heard the moans of his people in the wilderness and graciously sent manna and provided water from the rock by his power. God loved his people by routing Canaanite armies before them and giving them the promised land. The story of God in Israel is that God is loving and strong.

This is our story, too. It grounds our trust in God, even in the worst of circumstances. The work of God for his people did not begin and end with Israel. The work of God has continued since creation, and by his love and power God cares for his people and seeks to draw every human being into relationship with him. God is so sovereign over the world and so loving in his reach that he seeks relationship with everyone and uses the resources of his creation, even his fallen creation, to advance his goal of restored fellowship with humanity.

We trust in God's love and his power even though those two traits seem, at times, to conflict with each other. We all have experienced circumstances—whether through death, divorce, depression or disaster—where either the love or power of God were questioned. Questioning is natural; indeed, it is part of the story itself. Some question the love of God and conclude that perhaps there is no God at all or at least not one worth worshipping. Others question the power of God and postulate some kind of insuperable limitation upon divine sovereignty. Perhaps God can't, or worse, he can but won't.

The biblical story calls us to trust in both God's transcendent sovereignty (he can!) and in his immanent care (he loves!). The story calls us to trust that God is at work in everything for his purposes—at work to conform us to his image.

We know we do not understand. We know we cannot interpret God's acts in the world. We know we do not have all the answers to the difficult questions which love and sovereignty create for our myopic minds. Nevertheless, we trust. We trust the God of Israel and Jesus. He is our heavenly Father.

CONCLUSION

In the face of an emerging modernistic Deism among some southern Churches of Christ as well as some northern Disciples, Lipscomb and Harding affirmed the sovereign reign of God as an antidote to such "unbelief." They testified to the personal and dynamic involvement of God in the lives of Christians in contrast to the rationalistic impersonalism of God's mediated action. This is God's special provision for his people whereby he guides, cares and trains them for co-regency in the coming kingdom of God.

In contrast to an emerging view that limited God to his work through natural law and the written word, the NBST opposed any notion that God was absent from his world. Rather, God was always everywhere at work for the sake of his goal—to conform a people to the image of Christ who would dwell with him in the new heaven and new earth as co-regents. God is present in blessing and adversity to train, teach and test his people. God gives his people exactly what they need when they need it.

Though written in 1918 at the waning of the NBST, James Wells's hymn summarizes the faith orientation of Lipscomb and Harding. It has been a favorite in Churches of Christ—*perhaps* singing a theology that we have not always lived (or believed) but nevertheless commended to us by our spiritual forefathers.

I care not today what the morrow may bring,
If shadow or sunshine or rain,

The Lord I know ruleth o'er everything,
And all of my worries are vain.

Living by faith in Jesus above,
Trusting, confiding in His great love;
From all harm safe in His sheltering arm,
I'm living by faith and feel no alarm.[42]

DISCUSSION QUESTIONS

1. Given the suffering Lipscomb and Harding endured, what do you find encouraging, insensitive and/or enlightening about the quotes that head this chapter?

2. How do you understand Romans 8:28? In what ways has this text given meaning or hope in your life? Or, does the promise ring hollow because of your own experiences?

3. If you are able to perceive one, recount a moment in your own life where you "lived by faith" and saw the hand of God at work in your life. Reflect on its significance for your own story.

CHALLENGES

"Trust God and do good." This week identify a need in your community. Act in trust as you devote resources to that need that were previously dedicated to your comfort. This week choose another's need over your own wants. Trust that God will supply your need when the time comes.

PRAYER

Father, we believe, but help our unbelief. Train us to trust you. We acknowledge that you are the sovereign God and that you work in our lives for your purposes. Give us peace as we rest in your promises. Open our eyes to see what you are doing. Increase our faith that we might walk in your ways, leaning on you rather than our own understanding.

SUGGESTED READING

John Mark Hicks, *Yet Will I Trust Him: Understanding God in a Suffering World* (Joplin, MO: College Press, 1999).

Jean Baptiste Saint-Jure, *Trustful Surrender to Divine Providence: The Secret to Peace and Happiness* (Rockford, IL: Tan Books & Publishers, 1983).

Stephen Broyles, *The Wind that Destroys and Heals: Trusting the God of Sorrow and Joy* (Shaw Publishers, 2003).

FOUR

THE HOLY SPIRIT: GOD'S REDEMPTIVE PRESENCE IN THE WORLD

Does the Holy Spirit do anything now except what the Word does? Do we get help, any kind or in any way, from God except what we get by studying the Bible?...Does God answer our prayers by saying, 'Study the Bible?'
—James A. Harding (1902)[1]

Mark you, it does not matter how much you may read the Bible, nor how much you delight in it and go by it, this will not prevent the other train from smashing into yours, if there be no superhuman intervention—no overruling providence. I am so glad God has not withdrawn himself and left us to our own resources.
—James A. Harding (1905)[2]

Scripture does not teach that the Bible alone thoroughly furnishes the man of God for every good work, but that the Bible in addition to what had already been given does so....I am as far as the East is from the West from believing that neither God, Christ, nor the Holy Spirit can help us except by talking to us.
—James A. Harding (1906)[3]

When it comes to the work of the Holy Spirit, the Stone-Campbell Movement has been a veritable Dr. Jeckyl and Mr. Hyde. The Stone movement finds its beginnings in the celebrated Cane Ridge Revival, often called "America's Pentecost."[4] This revival witnessed holy singing, holy laughter, and people slain in the Spirit. Though some excesses occurred, Stone always believed the Spirit was powerfully involved as evidenced in its fruit—the demise of sectarianism.

The Campbells reacted strongly against the revivalism Stone embraced. Through his *Christian Baptist* Alexander Campbell led an assault on the prevailing views of the Holy Spirit. His lieutenant, Walter Scott, soon joined the foray with his influential *Discourse on the Holy Spirit.*[5] Their primary concern was the work of the Spirit in the conversion of the sinner. The Spirit did effect conversion, but he worked through the word rather than directly upon the human heart. By stressing the rationalistic side of the Christian message they hoped to provide assurance to many seekers who found themselves in the depths of despair on the anxious seat.

Unfortunately some did not distinguish between the Spirit's work in converting sinners and his work in comforting saints. Robert Richardson commented that some "reformers" had embraced an extreme doctrine claiming the "Holy Spirit stands for the 'Word of God,' by which they mean the scriptures." Yet these "word only" proclaimers had not explained whether a person could be said to be filled with the Spirit who, though fully acquainted with the Bible, fails to obey it?[6]

Despite efforts by Barton Stone, Robert Richardson and others, life in the Spirit was reduced to mere symbolism. Increasingly the power in the Christian life was will power and walking with the Lord a matter of ecclesiastical forms. Harding caught the mood when he wrote that many "stagger at the thought of the Holy Spirit entering into Christians and abiding in them." He continued that "they seem to think that he enters into them only in his Word, and he remains on the outside."[7]

A Spirit Dispute with J. C. Holloway

Timothy Weber notes that "American evangelicals historically had believed in an active, intervening God," who worked in days of old but also "continued to intervene in the lives of people in modern times."[8] Harding's overt supernaturalism focuses on the Holy Spirit who intervenes through special providence, responds to prayer, and is the power for kingdom living. It is difficult to overstate the importance placed on the Holy Spirit. Harding's contagious enthusiasm, according to Stanford Chambers, "drew and inspired a number and repelled others." Some students "had their spirituality deepened, and others in a measure became crystallized in a legalistic attitude."[9] J. N. Armstrong, R. H. Boll, R. C. Bell, and Stanford Chambers were among those captivated.[10]

Harding embraced a traditional, Stone-Campbell view of the Spirit in conversion (i.e., the Spirit does not work directly on the human heart). But with regard to the Christian, Harding's emphasis contrasted sharply with churches influenced by the *American Christian Review* and the *Firm Foundation.* Harding was so identified with this perspective that some believed the Bible schools founded by his students were theological innovators.[11]

By 1905, Dr. J. C. Holloway,[12] an Indiana physician, evangelist and editor, declared war on Harding's views. So strongly did the doctor object that he declared the "*Leader-Way* would be a much safer paper for young Christians to read" if Harding would shed his "semi-sectarian twaddle."[13]

Holloway wrote an eight-article series on the indwelling of the Holy Spirit. Over the course of the next year he, Harding, Boll, and others would exchange dozens of essays.[14] So persuasive were Holloway's articles for J. S. Warlick, renowned debater and editor, that he declared "Bro. Holloway is one of our strongest men and best writers."[15] Holloway's burden throughout was to prove that "no man today is led or influenced by the Holy Spirit" and that no one is indwelled by the "Holy Spirit as an entity."[16] That is, the Holy Spirit does not personally indwell Christians.

A potpourri of arguments were advanced that exalted human rationality and moral ability. Jesus said the "word" was the seed of the kingdom. There is no need for the indwelling Spirit because Christians could do a "hundred fold" with the Bible in their hand.[17] Because the Holy Spirit already "said all he is going to say, and done all he is going to do, for saint or sinner," Christians should not pray for preachers to be "guided." Rather God's revelation is like "mathematics" and those who rightly divide it need no illumination from the Spirit.[18]

Holloway's second major thrust is closely related to the previous one. The Bible is the infallible "all-sufficient" weapon given to Christians. "The Christian *lives* by the word of God; he *grows* by the word of God, and he is *saved* by the word of God," declared Holloway. Through this weapon the Christian can "slay the Adversary," and consequently, "no man now needs the personal indwelling of the Holy Spirit."[19] Indeed, the doctor argues that to "quench the Spirit to-day [sic] is to sneer at the Holy Scriptures" by affirming the need for spiritual help outside the written word of God. He declares "the Holy Scriptures…are in and of themselves, independent of all external helps, 'able to save your souls'."[20] Thus Dr. Holloway finally contended

> [T]hat since revelation was completed, the Spirit works through, in and by the Word as the only medium. My teaching inspires profound respect for the record of the Spirit as the Word of God. It gives the system of human redemption . . .a most rational aspect, and enables men to grasp it….Reduced to an epitome, it is this: THE HOLY SPIRIT IS THE ONLY AUTHENTIC AGENT, THE WORDS OF THE HOLY SPIRIT THE ONLY MEDIUM.[21]

It is little wonder that Holloway thought James A. Harding a danger. Holloway, in Harding's view, was an example of a rising deism among Churches of Christ. A "semi-infidelity possesses many," Harding writes, "which leads them to hold that the Father, Son and Holy Spirit have taken no active" role in the affairs of the world since the apostles. These ministers are in the habit of thinking the world "operate[s] like a clock wound up."[22] Holloway's perspective taught that God made the world and subjected it to law by which it continued to run without any further intervention from him.[23] Harding forcefully rejected this. It was Satan, Harding declared, who teaches that "God made this world and subjected it to law."[24]

Harding's apocalyptic worldview held a grave sense of failure before

God and a relatively pessimistic understanding of human moral ability. Ruminating on Romans 7, Harding confesses:

> "What I would I do not." I would do right, that is I desire, to do the very thing that Jesus would do were he in my place, and to do it just as he would do it. Alas! how wretchedly I fail in doing the thing I would: If I preach, I am not satisfied with my sermon…if a brother leads the prayers, I am apt to find my mind wandering off to other matters, so I do not pray as I should: In fact it is probable that I do nothing perfectly, just as Jesus would do it were he in my place.[25]

Harding denied human moral ability to do "right." "Who does not know that he is unable to care for himself, to guide, to guard and to strengthen himself?" Harding asks.[26] Some argued that Christians simply were to do the best they could. But Harding claimed he never had met the person "who does the best" they know. "What we need is a Savior to save people who have not done the best they knew, to save sinners."[27]

The Holy Spirit in Harding's theology was the Christian's enabler. The Spirit is the secret to living in the shadow of the second coming. The Spirit is to the Christian what electricity is to the street car or sap to the tree. Electricity, Harding believed, was mysterious. You can't see it but its power was nearly unlimited. Without that unseen power the trolley may be pretty but it is nothing but a hulk of rusting iron. So the Christian without the Spirit coursing through her being is a lifeless shell.[28]

Harding pitied those embracing Holloway's deism:

> I feel sorry for those who are afflicted by these dreadful, blighting, semi-infidel materialistic notions, that leave God, Christ, the Holy Spirit…wholly out of the Christian's life—for those who think all spiritual beings left us when the Bible was finished, and who think that we now have to fight the battle

> alone. Some of these people pray, but what they pray for is more than I can tell, unless it is for the 'reflex influence.'[29]

Harding had profound respect for Scripture. It was a means of grace that mediated an encounter with the Father. But he rejected Holloway's argument that Scripture *alone* was sufficient to the Christian's health. Knowledge of the word of God was important, but Harding asked, "has not Dr. Holloway yet learned that we need more than knowledge?"[30] Christians need wisdom, power and love for living in God's kingdom, things that come only through Holy Spirit in response to prayer. "Mark you," wrote Harding, "it does not matter how much you may read the Bible, nor how much you delight in it." This will not keep Christians from stumbling. God strengthens "with power through his Spirit in the inward man."[31]

Though Holloway intended to honor God's word as a divine gift to humanity, he actually undermines that word by denying the Father's other gifts to disciples. The Spirit is here to aid and guide Christians. Perhaps nothing, however, could have prepared Holloway for Harding's bold assertion that "scripture does not teach that the Bible alone thoroughly furnishes the man of God for every good work." Rather, "the Bible in addition to what had already been given" equips disciples for life in the kingdom.[32] Soldiers are not issued a single implement nor are disciples. Scripture complements the other weapons granted to Christians. The indwelling Spirit is such a weapon in the saint's arsenal for battle against the spiritual forces of evil. As R. H. Boll pointed out to the Indiana editor, Christians receive not only Christ's teaching but Jesus himself, through the Spirit, to walk alongside us.[33] God gave Scripture but he also gave himself in the Holy Spirit.

Harding's years of immersion in the Bible assured him that Holloway was a Sadducee, knowing neither the power of God nor his word.[34] God had always dwelled with his people. It was God through his angel who was Helper, Comforter and Guide in the wilderness. God through his angel met with Joshua and God's angel dwelled with Israel in the days of the Judges (Judges 2:1-5). Thus, Harding concludes that "God dwelt among his people, under the old covenant, to guide and guard, to strengthen and comfort them."[35]

The tabernacle and temple were "preparatory to and typical of the much grander building" of God's church.[36] God dwelt among his people through his angel but now, however, God dwells *in* his people through his Spirit. Contrary to what Holloway claimed, the Comforter has been granted to all who believe. Harding cited his favorite Spirit text:

> If any man thirst, let him come unto me and drink. He that believeth on me, as the scripture hath said, from within him shall flow rivers of living waters. By this spake he of the Spirit which they that believe on him were to receive: for the Spirit was not yet given because Jesus was not yet glorified. (John 7:37-39)[37]

Who is to receive the Spirit, asked Harding rhetorically? "Jesus answers: 'Any man,' 'He that believeth on me.'"[38]

The Harding-Holloway discussion fizzled out as the doctor began a new journal, *Defender of the Word*, and published a book, *The Spirit and the Word.* The journal and the book were aimed specifically at countering Harding's influence on the Holy Spirit. Harding only confirmed Holloway's suspicions that he was a "mystical" dreamer[39] playing fast and loose with the word of God.

> I felt sure you would keep nibbling at that hook until you would find yourself swinging in midair; and, sure enough, you have now committed yourself so that you can never get loose only by renouncing your foggy ideas and resolving to be content with the written word of God.[40]

Harding, for his part, believed Holloway was equally deadly to those striving to live in the shadow of the second coming. He lamented:

> I do not know any doctrine taught by any of the Protestant sectarian bodies that is more flatly contradictory of the gen-

> eral tenor of Scripture…that is a more blighting, withering, deadly curse to those that believe it, than Dr. Holloway's doctrine….I firmly believe he rightly curses every man whom he induces to believe it.[41]

For Harding the indwelling Spirit was a profound mystery to be embraced in faith. Dr. Holloway eschewed the mysterious and embraced a religious secularism.

There was more to this discussion than the Holy Spirit. Harding and Holloway locked horns on special providence, grace and prayer, whether the Sermon on the Mount was addressed to Christians—all key themes in the NBST. This forgotten battle between these two giants is significant because it was one of the first assaults on the apocalyptic worldview in Churches of Christ. Holloway's view, by the 1930s, would emerge as the dominant tradition.

The God who Seeks Intimate Communion

Scripture declares that God is relational. The one God exists as Father, Son, and Holy Spirit in perpetual communion. Reading the biblical narrative through the lens of the apocalyptic worldview, as Harding noted, illuminates this theme. The metaphors used in the narrative are often breathtakingly suggestive of the intimate relationship into which disciples are called. God is a loving Father wounded by his son's rejection (Hos 11:1-11). God is a passionate Husband seeking to reclaim his wayward wife (Hos 2:14-16; Ezek 16). Isaiah dares to say God is like a nursing mother who comforts her child (Isa 66:13: cf. 7-8, 12).

The narrative of Scripture reinforces the longing of God for relationship with his creation. He created humanity in his image to share in the divine fellowship. When humanity rejected that fellowship through Adam's rebellion, the God revealed as father, husband and mother did not give up on the goal. Thus when God redeemed Israel from slavery he determined to dwell with them as his people. Sin was not too high a hurdle for God to overcome for the sake of being with his loved ones. Isaiah testifies to Yahweh's gracious presence with Israel:

> "Surely they are my people,
> sons who will not be false to me";
> and so he became their Savior.
> In all their distress he too was distressed,
> and the angel of his presence saved them.
> In his love and mercy he redeemed them
> he lifted them and carried them all the days of old . . .
> Where is he who set his Holy Spirit among them . . .
> They were given rest by the Spirit of the Lord.
> This is how you guided your people
> to make for yourself a glorious name. (Isa 63:8-9, 11c, 14)

God dwelled with his people, giving them visible demonstrations of his loving fellowship with them. His glory filled the tabernacle (Ex 40:34-38) and the temple (2 Chr 5:13b-14; 7:1-2). More than mere symbolism was involved in God's dwelling:

> I will put my dwelling among you, and I will not abhor you. I will walk among you and be your God, and you will be my people. I am the Lord your God, who brought you out of Egypt so that you would no longer be slaves. (Lev 26:12-13a)

Following the exile the rebuilt temple was but a shadow of Solomon's, yet Haggai assures the people that God's Spirit remained with them (Hag 2:5; cf. 1:13; 2:4). The testimony of the Old Testament is that Israel was born, delivered, established, nurtured and sustained by God's Holy Spirit.[42]

Despite Yahweh's gracious presence with his people, Israel found herself utterly unable to live up to the covenant of love. As in the garden before, the pollution of Israel drove the holy presence of God from the temple (Ezek 10). But the passionate Husband of Israel longed for not only a restoration of relationship but a deepening of it. Thus the prophets had visions of an even richer covenant with the Lord, a covenant in which sins would be extinguished and God's own

Spirit would be placed "in you" (Ezek 36:25-27; cf. John 14:17). Joel promised that God would pour out his Spirit on all people. Not just prophets or powerful men but also on the "servants, both men and women, I will pour out my Spirit in those days" (Joel 2:28-29). The age to come was to be an age of the Spirit and God's people were to be a community of the Spirit.

Jesus realized Israel's messianic and spiritual hopes. The Gospel writers describe Jesus as the Spirit-bearer (John 3:34; Luke 4:18-19).[43] The Spirit is connected to his birth (Luke 1:35). The Spirit equips Jesus with power for service at his baptism (Luke 3:21-22; 4:14); Jesus grants the Spirit to those who have faith in him; he brings the Holy Spirit as "streams of living water," to quench the thirst for the parched soul (John 4:14; 7:37-39). Just as he was born and baptized of the Spirit, so those entering into God's new community will be born and baptized of the Spirit (John 3:5; 1 Cor 12:12-13; Titus 3:5).

The Old Testament had foreseen a connection between possession of the Holy Spirit and doing God's will (Ezek 36:27). Indeed, the Spirit is the life of the community of faith (Ezek 37:1-14). So Jesus promises the Spirit as a Teacher, Guide, and Counselor to his disciples (John 14:25-27; 1 John 2:20, 27).

The book of Acts bears witness to a Spirit-endowed, Spirit-empowered, and Spirit-led community. The Holy Spirit empowered disciples for witness (Acts 4:8, 31; 7:55). The Spirit guided evangelists to seekers (Acts 8:29, 39) and closed doors for others (Acts 16:6-7). The Spirit shattered the race barrier erected by disciples (Acts 10:19-48; 15:8). The Spirit initiated the Gentile mission of Paul and Barnabas (Acts 13:2). Spirit-led disciples cared for the Grecian widows (Acts 6:3). The Holy Spirit appointed disciples as elders (Acts 20:28). Having the Spirit was the mark of an authentic disciple (Acts 19:2). The Spirit filled the church with joy (Acts 13:52) by strengthening and encouraging her (Acts 9:31). The Spirit was given to all those who obeyed God (Acts 5:32). The church is nothing, in Luke's view, if it is not the community of the Holy Spirit.

The epistles reinforce the picture painted by Luke. The church created by the Spirit was the fellowship of the Spirit.[44] Paul draws on the Old Testament imagery of God dwelling with his people in the temple, announcing that God continues to indwell his temple, the church. "[Y]ou too are being built together to become a dwelling in which God lives by his Spirit" (Eph 2:22).

God's temple is a place for family. The image of believers as God's family (Eph 2:19; 1 Tim 3:15) flows naturally from Paul's reference to God as Father. It is the Father, through his Spirit, who fosters intimacy.

> For all who are led by the Spirit of God are children of God. For you did not receive a spirit of slavery to fall back into fear, but you have received a spirit of adoption. When we cry, 'Abba! Father!' it is that very Spirit bearing witness with our spirit that we are children of God (Rom 8:14b-16)

> And because you are children, God has sent the Spirit of his Son into our hearts, crying "Abba! Father!" So you are no longer a slave but a child, and if a child then also an heir, through God. (Gal 4:6-7)

Jesus taught his disciples to call the Creator God "Abba" (Mark 14:36).[45] Through the Holy Spirit, Christians have the same intimate access to our Abba as Jesus of Nazareth. Indeed, the daring prayer language of Jesus is evidence, for Paul, of the indwelling Spirit.

Paul writes to disciples who have accepted the gospel message, possess the Old Testament, and are reading the letter we call "Ephesians." Yet, Paul intercedes on their behalf, requesting divine intervention beyond the sacred page. After assuring them they had been "sealed" with Spirit (Eph 1:13) as a "guarantee" (Eph 1:14) of their inheritance, Paul asked that

> The God of our Lord Jesus Christ, the glorious Father, may give you the Spirit of wisdom and revelation, so that you may know him better. I pray also that the eyes of your heart may

> be enlightened in order that you may know the hope to which he has called you. (Eph 1:17-18, NIV)

Paul prays that the Spirit "enlighten" the Ephesians regarding their "inheritance" and the divine "power" working within them. Paul did not pray that the Ephesians would memorize his letter. He prays that the "glorious Father" would unleash his Spirit for the sake of ever deepening relationship. Paul does not pray that they will know more about God but that they might know—that is, experience—him. It is a cry for intimacy.

Paul prayed for Christians. Spiritual forces, the powers and principalities, want to destroy God's colony of believers (Eph 6:12). Mere human fortitude would not ensure survival but divine intervention does. So Paul laid three requests before the throne of God (Eph 3:14-19). First, that God would "strengthen [them] with power through his Spirit in your inner being" (Eph 3:16). Divine power is granted through the instrumentality of the Spirit. Second, Paul prays for more "power." This power is directed toward communally experiencing the infinite depth of God's love. Third, Paul prays that Christians experience a love that "surpasses knowledge" so they can be "filled to the measure of all the fullness of God" (Eph 3:19).

God's colonial outpost, the church, lives as a witness, in the present, of things to come. Through Christ we have experienced resurrection, though we still face death. Because of Golgotha we have salvation, yet we wait in hope for the revelation of our redemption. We have the "first fruits" (Rom 8:23) of the Spirit as God's pledge of the rest of the harvest. The indwelling is a foretaste of what God has planned for his family. Harding believed that in the *eschaton* Christians will receive the baptism of the Holy Spirit that Christ had received. "I believe it [Spirit baptism] will be granted to all the righteous in the everlasting kingdom of God."[46] The indwelling points us to a restoration of full communion with the triune God in the new Jerusalem.

LIVING IN THE SPIRIT

Keeping in step with the Spirit is something we often fail to do. It is far easier to trust in our senses and abilities than to lean upon God's invisible Guest. Yet we believe that if we are to thrive as children of God we must embrace the Father's gift and surrender to the Spirit.

Basking in His Presence

A simple suggestion may help us open up to life in the Spirit. Learn to enjoy God. The Psalmists exhort us to "delight yourself in the Lord" (37:4) and "taste and see that the Lord is good" (34:8). The call is not to study God, sacrifice for God, or even obey God, but delight in God. Take pleasure in God. Fall in love with God. As we long for him, the God of holy relationships will embrace us through his indwelling Spirit. The Spirit is God's means of personal intimacy with his family. Prayer and worship, as means of being filled with the Spirit, bring us into intimate communion with the triune God as a foretaste of the new creation.

Longing for Transformation

The indwelling Spirit releases Christians from the bankruptcy of moralism and legalism. Christians struggle today, as Israel did before, with worldly compromise. The key to kingdom ethics is the Spirit living in redeemed aliens (Gal 5:16). Life is brought about by the Spirit. Since Christians "live by the Spirit" they are "guided by the Spirit" (Gal 5:25). Mere legal righteousness does not satisfy the longing of disciples. The hunger of the Christian heart is transformation. Through the power of God's Spirit we long for a restoration of the very image of God that is defaced through human rebellion.

In the process of transformation the indwelling Spirit helps our infirmities. Harding said "a book can not pray or groan" on our behalf.[47] But the Spirit knowing us intimately; he knows exactly what to pray to bring about our renewal. Christians are often unsure about their daily walk and ministries. He leads us through those circumstances (Acts

16:10).[48] He guides us through the community of faith (Acts 13:1-3). He directs us through Scripture. He transforms us in the garden of prayer.

Equipped for Ministry

The Holy Spirit does not just bind us to the Lover of our souls and transform us into the image of Christ; the Spirit also equips us for ministry in this fallen world. Ministry does not have to be conceived as preaching. The most "mundane" tasks should be viewed as sacrificial service to the Lord. Artistry and craftsmanship were spiritual gifts given to Bezalel and Oholiab to design and construct the tabernacle (Ex 31:1-6; 35:30-36:1). As the church struggles with its alien status in the world we continue to pray that he gift his people until we attain the goal (Eph 4:13).

CONCLUSION

Though surviving in pockets in the Churches of Christ, Harding's perspective was soon eclipsed by rationalistic and symbolic views. Some of Harding's students recoiled at his insistence that Christianity is a divine-human encounter. R. L. Whiteside, called the "David Lipscomb of Texas," rejected his teacher's theology. For him there could be no divine aid apart from the written word.[49] "Peter affirms," wrote Whiteside, "that we have in the Bible everything that pertains to life and godliness." Therefore "to pray for a power or a means of godliness or spiritual life separate and apart from the Bible" is to cast reproach upon God's word.[50] So marginalized had the Spirit become that Whiteside often spoke as easily of the "fruit of the word" as he did the "fruit of the Spirit."[51] Those who looked for additional aid from God "speak fluently of the insufficiency of the word of God."[52]

H. Leo Boles, likewise, embraced a representative indwelling of God's Spirit. Taking a page out of Holloway's playbook, he asked, "How does the Spirit comfort and give hope to God's people?" His answer: only through the "revealed word." The Spirit can only be said to indwell Christians symbolically. God and Christ dwell in Christians through his representative, the Spirit; likewise, "the Holy Spirit dwells in us through his agent, the word of truth." "To yield to the simple teachings of the New Testament," Boles declares, is to be "led by the Holy Spirit."[53]

We believe that Scripture is Spirit-breathed. We believe that the word should be read more not less. But if Churches of Christ are to take the Bible seriously then we must take what it says about the Spirit seriously. Perhaps we have been asking the wrong question. Perhaps the question is not, "Does the Spirit operate separate and apart from the word?" but "Does the word work separate and apart from the Spirit?" (cf. 2 Cor. 3:6). The word is an implement of the Spirit not the other way around. We believe Harding's spiritual legacy provides great resources for recovering the power of the Spirit for the church today.

DISCUSSION QUESTIONS

1. How representative are Holloway's teachings on the Holy Spirit in your experience? How representative is Harding's?

2. Is God fundamentally a relational being? How does the indwelling Spirit facilitate an intimate relationship with God? Do you delight in God?

3. How is the indwelling Spirit an antidote to moralism and legalism? What does it mean to be led by the Spirit?

CHALLENGES

Personalize Paul's prayers in Ephesians (1:15-21; 3:14-19) and pray them for yourself and your congregation.

Imagine the passionate God "alluring" you into the desert where you learn to call God "my husband" rather than merely "my master" (Hos 2:14-16).

Engage the Song of Songs on a contemplative level as if it were an allegory of God's passionate love for you and your congregation.

PRAYER

Open our eyes, Father, as you did Elisha's servant, to know we are surrounded by your gracious Presence. Grant us your Spirit of wisdom and revelation that we may come to experience you and the hope to which you have called us. Grant us power, through your Spirit, in our inner being to walk as Jesus walked, to love as Jesus loved, and to bless as Jesus blessed. Amen.

RESOURCES

C. Leonard Allen and Danny Gray Swick, *Participating in God's Life: Two Crossroads for Churches of Christ* (Orange, CA: New Leaf, 2001).

Gordon D. Fee, *Paul, the Spirit, and the People of God* (Peabody, MA: Hendrickson, 1996)

Michael Green, *I Believe in the Holy Spirit*, Revised (Grand Rapids: Eerdmans, 2004)

Randall J. Harris, *The Contemporaries Meet the Classics on the Holy Spirit* (West Monroe, LA: Howard, 2004)

Dallas Willard, *The Divine Conspiracy: Rediscovering Our Hidden Life in God* (San Francisco: HarperSanFrancisco, 1998).

PART II

KINGDOM SPIRITUALITY: FOUR MEANS OF GRACE

They devoted themselves to the apostles' teaching and to the fellowship, to the breaking of bread and to prayer.
Acts 2:42 (NIV)

Our greatest trouble now is, it seems to me, a vast unconverted membership. A very large percent of the church members among us seem to have very poor conceptions of what a Christian ought to be. They are brought into the church during these high-pressure protracted meetings, and they prove to be a curse instead of a blessing. They neglect prayer, the reading of the Bible, and the Lord's day meetings, and, of course, they fail to do good day by day as they should. Twelve years of continuous travel among the churches have forced me to the sad conclusion that a very small number of the nominal Christians are worthy of the name.
—James A. Harding (1887)[1]

As a summary of early Christian steadfastness, Acts 2:42 has served as an influential reference point in the Believer's Church tradition but it has been especially important to the Stone-Campbell Movement. As early as the 1830s some even regarded it as the biblical "order of worship." Others continued that perspective into the early twentieth century.[2] Harding, however, believed these "four duties" were listed "in the order of their importance."[3]

Harding identified the four as (1) reading and studying the Bible, (2) ministering to others (especially the poor) as we share ("fellowship") our resources, (3) participating in the Lord's day meeting at the Lord's table, and (4) habitual prayer. Sometimes Harding identified all of these activities with the Lord's day,[4] but generally understood Bible study, ministering to the poor, and prayers as daily spiritual disciplines. Believers should read their Bibles daily, "do good" daily as they have opportunity, and pray every morning, noon, afternoon and evening.

But these are no mere "duties." Rather, they are "four great means of grace"—appointed means by which God dynamically acts among, in and through his people.[5] They are not avenues of human self-reliance but modes of divine transformation through which God graciously sanctifies believers. They are spiritual disciplines by which God conforms his people to the image of Christ.

Harding emphasized that the "life of a successful Christian is a continual growth in purity, a constant changing into a complete likeness to Christ."[6] To "grow more and more into the likeness of Christ" should be the Christian's greatest desire.[7] In other words, Harding believed discipleship was the central dimension of the kingdom of God. Consequently, one of the dangers of revivalism ("protracted meetings") was the immediate interest in a large number of conversions where the main concern was "escaping hell and getting into heaven" as opposed to discipling people to lead "lives of absolute consecration to the Lord." As a result, these "converts are much more anxious to be saved than they are to follow Christ."[8]

Harding's antidote was to recommend the "four habits" of Acts 2:42 as expressions of both communal and individual piety. Whoever neglects them will falter and their "falling away is sure."[9] But if one will pursue these spiritual practices, "he will surely abide in Christ. These four are God's means of grace to transform a poor, frail, sinful human being into the likeness of Christ." Whoever "faithfully uses these means unto the end of life can not [*sic*] be lost." Specifically, in response to the question, "Will God hold us responsible for little mistakes?" Harding answered: God "holds nothing against us" whether we sinned "in ignorance, weakness or willfulness" as long as we live in Christ as people who faithfully practice these spiritual disciplines.[10]

The divine dynamic is graciously active through these communal and individual faith-practices by the power of the Holy Spirit. God actively transforms his people into his own image and believers who pursue these gifts of grace will experience that transformation by divine power rather than by human effort.

FIVE

LISTENING TO GOD: READING SCRIPTURE

"The most important thing in the world is daily, diligent, prayerful study of the divine word."
—James A. Harding (1908)[1]

"There is a crying need of Bible study, and faithful study will bring its own sweet reward. There is such a joy of discovery (Psalm 119:162), such a quickening of zeal, enlargement of the spiritual horizon, strengthening of faith and courage, and renewing of the mind, as could never come by mere listening to sermons or reading of religious books and articles."
—Robert H. Boll (1910)[2]

In 1909 the Disciples of Christ gathered at the Centennial Convention in Pittsburg, Pennsylvania to celebrate the one hundredth anniversary of Thomas Campbell's *Declaration and Address.* There Walter Scott Priest representatively expressed the public self-image of the movement. "We have always been," he said, "distinctly and peculiarly, people of *the Book*—the Bible."[3]

Though the Churches of Christ did not participate in the convention, none would have disagreed with Priest's characterization except they might have contested whether it still applied to the Disciples. To say that we are a "people of the book" was as common place as other mottos within Churches of Christ, most of which symbolize our allegiance to "the book." We pursued a hermeneutic that intended "to speak where the Bible speaks and be silent where the Bible is silent." We claimed that we had "no creed, but Christ" (which meant that the Bible is our creed). We sought to "call Bible things by Bible names." The Bible was the foundation of our faith and the focus of our corporate life as a people.

However, it would be a mistake to construe this as a form of "bibliolatry"—a worship of the Bible. Rather, the best of our tradition regarded the Bible as a means of grace; a means towards the goal of transformation into the image of Christ and communion with God. For example, even though Alexander Campbell pioneered a scientific reading of the Bible within the movement, he believed that one "reads the Book of God to commune with God."[4] We read the Bible, Harding insists, "that we may know" God.[5] Or, as Priest remarked, believers are not merely interested in the historical and literary data within Scripture, but we "seek to know the deep purposes of God."[6] In other words, through Bible reading, we "listen to God."

HARDING ON BIBLE READING

When Harding died in 1922, Boll eulogized his mentor as one who "set more people *to reading the Bible*...than any other preacher; and he infused his own love and appreciation of the Word into those who came under his sway."[7] As an Associate Editor of the *Gospel Advocate* (1883-1890), Harding encouraged the daily reading of three and a third chapters as a spiritual discipline in order to read the whole Bible in one year.[8] He formed Bible reading classes wherever he went as an itinerant evangelist and collected "Bible reading cards" which detailed commitments and progress.[9] He believed the "chief duty of the teacher in the Church [is] to lead people to the daily, diligent, prayerful study of the Word," and he devoted "more time and energy to that one point than to any other."[10]

In the first issue of his own periodical *The Way*, Harding characteristically stressed that reading the Bible was the "most important duty of life."[11] Consequently, he believed "a taste for Bible reading must be cultivated."[12] This begins in the home with families but extends to private study and the public reading of Scripture on the Lord's Day. The mutual edification of the assembly was focused on the reading and exposition of Scripture. For Harding, Scripture was the air we breathe and our daily nourishment. It was, as Harding put it, the "first rule of success" in Christian living.[13]

This may seem an overstatement, especially if we hear it as a legalism. Indeed, where postmodernity stresses relationality and experience, reading a book seems a rather distant concern. But this would be to misunderstand the importance that Harding attached to daily Bible reading. The goal was relationality through exposure to the mind of God in Scripture. Since "God is the author of the Bible, we should read it that we may know him."[14]

Bible reading, according to Harding, shapes a people into the image of Christ. Reading with a prayerful attitude matures believers and forms them into wise disciples of Christ.

> What inefficient preachers, elders, deacons and churches need above all other things are faith, knowledge and wisdom. The diligent, persistent study of the Word, combined with a whole-hearted continuous, prayerful effort to walk therein, will supply the knowledge and develop the faith; and then one is in the proper condition of mind and heart to pray for wisdom, and to receive it in answer to his prayer.[15]

Christians read the Bible, then, toward the end of knowing God through a mature, lived faith. Through reading, we experience God and progressively conform our thoughts and life to God's purposes.

To preachers he recommended his own habit of spending "four to six hours per day for the study of the word."[16] And he suggested that all Christians read the Bible through every year. Harding divided the number of pages in his Old Testament by 365 and the number of pages in his New Testament by 182. By reading four pages each day, he would read the Old Testament once and the New Testament twice each year.[17] Or, alternatively, by reading three and a third chapters a day or three from the Old Testament and one from the New, one would read the whole Bible every year.[18]

Harding practiced what he preached. In 1903 Harding claimed that for twenty years he had read the Old Testament at least once and the New Testament twice each year, and sometimes read "through the entire Book twice, three times, four times, and in one year [had] read the Old Testament through five times and the New six."[19] As of 1914, Harding had read the former sixty times and the latter one hundred and thirty times.[20]

Harding was particularly concerned to emphasize two dimensions of Bible reading. Methodologically, he thought consecutive, regular reading of the text was more beneficial than concordance topical study. One of the reasons deistic opposition to special providence was on the rise, according to Harding, was that "the entire Bible" was not "studied regularly and consecutively."[21] Further, "partisans," he wrote, favor concordance or topical study because "they enjoy discussion rather than worship." Texts become points of argument rather than an entrée into the mind and heart of God. The person who stresses topical study "can never have the broad, full, and comprehensive appreciation" of the divine story that is available through reading the Bible from beginning to end.[22]

Devotionally, he regarded prayerful Bible reading as worship—a means of grace, that is, a means by which God encounters us and strengthens us. Bible reading is dynamic rather than static. God is active rather than passive. It is a divine-human encounter. Consequently, Bible reading involved delightful meditation. Harding counseled that readers should occasionally "pause" to reflect on what they had read and delight in it.[23]

A Theology of Scripture

Embedded within the unfolding redemptive-historical story in Scripture is the expectation that the covenantal texts will be publicly read and communally appropriated. Near the end of the Torah is the regulation that every seven years all Israel was to assemble to hear the reading of the law "so that they can listen and learn to fear the LORD your God and follow carefully all the words of this law" (Deut 31:11-12). On several occasions in the history of Israel all the people gathered to hear the law read as a form of covenant renewal (Josh 8:33-35; 2 Chr 34:30-32; Neh 8:1-9:3). After the exile, Jewish believers weekly read from the law and the prophets in their synagogues (cf. Luke 4:16-21; Acts 13:14-15; 15:21).

The primary context of the New Testament documents is public reading. Paul's letters, for example, were intended to be read to the assembled church (cf. 1 Thes 5:27; Col 4:16; cf. Rev 1:3). Paul urged Timothy to "devote [himself] to the public reading of Scripture" (1 Tim 4:13). When the church gathered, the law and the prophets were read (the Bible of the early church) and the writings of the apostles were also read. This has been the historic practice of the church throughout the centuries. For example, continuing New Testament practices, assembled Christians in the second century, according to Justin Martyr (ca. 155 A.D.), read from "the memoirs of the apostles or the writings of the prophets" every Sunday "as long as time permit[ted]."[24]

Also embedded within these covenant documents is the example of personal, private engagement with texts. The Psalmist, for example, characterizes the blessed person as the one whose "delight is in the law of the Lord, and on his law he meditates day and night" (Ps 1:2). Psalm 119 is the classic expression of this personal devotion to the word of God. Timothy's mother and grandmother nurtured his faith through a knowledge of "the holy Scriptures" (2 Tim 3:15; cf. 2 Tim 1:5).

Scripture's power is located in its divine witness and its profitability. The testimony of Scripture is divine testimony. It is "God-breathed" (2 Tim 3:16). Through human messengers—writing with all their human resources and abilities—God bears witness to his work, interprets it, and applies it to the specific communities which Scripture addresses. Scripture thereby equips God's people for service.

God created community for his people and entered into covenant with them. Led by God's covenantal messengers (whether Moses, the prophets or the apostles), the community heard the word of the Lord through those messengers. That word bore witness to the mighty acts of God (Creation, Exodus, Incarnation, Resurrection) and interpreted their meaning. But these interpretations did not arise out of their own imagination; they were given by revelation (Eph 3:2-6; 2 Pet 2:20-21). Those messages applied the meaning of God's mighty acts in the community of God. The record of this witness is the church's Scripture—the writings of the prophets and apostles. Scripture is applied theology, a divine voice in a human wilderness.

Scripture functions, then, as a covenant document to equip the people of God for service to the world and to guide their path toward embodying the presence of God in the world (2 Tim 3:16). Through reading Scripture we seek to understand the mystery of God's redemptive work (cf. Eph 3:2-6). We enter the mind of God in Christ and see the world with God's eyes. Scripture is our interpretative framework for understanding our place in God's story. It is a pair of glasses, a set of lenses, we put on to see the world rightly. Wearing these lenses we are disciplined by the testimony of the word and guided by its values. By reading we embrace God's story and learn to interpret our experience through God's kingdom plans and purposes.

But this process is not mechanical. Of course, there are "rules of interpretation" since Scripture is given to us in human language situated in a particular human culture addressing human contexts. Alexander Campbell, for example, insisted that Scripture should be read just like we read any other document—human hermeneutical rules apply.[25] But if we reduce reading the Bible to mere human mechanics then we will diminish its spiritual power.

The presence of the Holy Spirit is a necessary dimension of Bible reading. Even as scientific a reader as Alexander Campbell recognized that if we are "to receive any benefit" from reading the Scriptures, "we must earnestly pray for the Spirit to apply them and to explain them to our hearts."[26] The Spirit accompanies the word in such a way that the Spirit works in the hearts of its readers. It is through reading Scripture that we "feel the Spirit of God working in [us] to will and do every thing pleasing to God."[27]

Reading Scripture, whether publicly as a community or privately as individuals, is a dynamic process by which the words on the page interact with the human mind in the power of the Spirit. Through the reading, meditation and teaching of Scripture, God clarifies his purposes for his people (cf. 2 Tim 2:7; Phil 3:15; Acts 15:28). God is no mere spectator when we read; rather he seeks us, just as we seek him.

> The man of God reads the Book of God to commune with God, "*to feel after him and find him,*" to feel his power and his divinity stirring within him; to have his soul fired, quickened, animated by the spirit of grace and truth. He reads the Bible to enjoy the God of the Bible.... Such a one converses with God as one who speaks by signs. His readings are heavenly musings. God speaks: he listens.[28]

This dynamic understanding of Bible reading grounds the ultimate goal of Bible reading—a means of grace (sanctification) by which God actively transforms people into his own image. God comes to us through his word in authority (norms and standards), but also in power (transforming us by the Spirit) and in presence (fellowship). The word—in conjunction with the Spirit—informs our intellect but also transforms our affections and empowers our wills. The goal of Bible reading is transformation into the likeness of Christ by the power of the Spirit.

THE PRACTICE OF BIBLE READING

Churches of Christ have always stressed reading the Bible. Many churches encourage reading the entire Bible every year through various programs. Bible classes are a staple among Churches of Christ. Rarely will you find a Church of Christ without them, and, of course, the teaching of the word is a central focus in the corporate worship of the church. The Bible is not a neglected book among us.

Or is it? The public reading of Scripture is relatively rare except as part of a sermon. Some question whether our Bible classes function more as supportive self-help groups rather than places of serious Bible study. Biblical illiteracy is on the rise and has reached alarming proportions.[29] There is a tremendous need for a renewal of Bible reading, study and meditation among our people—both as individuals and as communities.

We suggest three approaches to the practice of Bible reading. Not all reading is the same. We do not read a newspaper the way we read a poem, nor do we read a novel the way we read a billboard. Below we suggest that every believer and the believing community as a whole read the Bible in three ways: as a story, as a rich source of meaning, and as a text for silent meditation. These are three ways to "listen to God" both individually and communally.

Story

Harding emphasized reading the Bible "consecutively" or, to put it in more contemporary terms, as a narrative or story. The Bible has a plot—it is the unfolding drama of God's creative and redemptive work. It is the story of his restoration project—to restore the *shalom* of his original creation through redeeming the fallen world.

To read Scripture as narrative is to read it in the framework of its overarching plot. It is to expose ourselves to its language and values, to discern the world it communicates, and to embrace the story as our own. Through narrative reading we enter into the world of Scripture in such a way that it absorbs our own world. We begin to see our world in the light of God's creation, redemptive intent, and ultimate restoration. We see what the world should be. Harding read the whole Bible so often because he wanted to live in that story—to participate in the drama of redemption. Constant, daily reading shapes the heart and mind with the language and values of the biblical story.

In our multi-media age, we are subtly shaped and formed by the images we see and read. Teens that grew up watching "Friends" on television were subtly shaped by the values of that sitcom. Such "stories" sink into our hearts in unconscious ways and before we realize it we are living out those stories. Our exposure to the varied stories of culture shape us.

Reading the Bible as a story, and reading it daily in large chunks (much like we read a novel) counteracts the narrative of fallen culture. Daily Bible reading is a counter-cultural act—it situates us over against fallen culture. Through it we imbibe a different story that has radically different values than the one in which we live as fallen human beings. The different texts of Scripture blend to form a symphony which finds its crescendo in the incarnation, ministry, crucifixion and resurrection of Jesus—events which prefigure the fullness of the kingdom of God in the new heaven and new earth.

There is a great need to renew the reading of Scripture in our assemblies. We can only embrace the story as a community when we hear it read in large chunks as a community. Certainly, the Lord's Supper, our praises and our prayers do this as well, but we need also to hear the word as a community.

Believers who do not know what the word "exegesis" means are discipled by their constant reading of the word as narrative. Such reading does not produce scholars in the academic sense, but it does produce disciples.[30]

Study

The church needs readers first, but it also needs serious students and scholars. Reading Scripture as a student focuses on the meaning of specific texts. It pursues what is known as the "historical-grammatical" method. This approach reads Scripture in the context of its own historical situation and pays close attention to the language of the text. It is the stuff of which academic commentaries are made, that is, exegesis—the discipline that draws out the meaning of a text.

This historical or critical reading of Scripture seeks to understand what the original author meant when he wrote the text. This involves an appreciation of the historical context of the document, the culture in which it was written, the meaning of the language in that context, and what problem/situation it was addressing. Such understanding guides us in applying biblical theology in the present. What the text meant to its original readers guides our understanding of what it means for us today.

Exegesis asks the questions who, what, where, when and why. The student analyzes, parses and dissects the text. What did Paul mean when he said that Christ "emptied himself" (Phil 2:7)? What does the word "empty" mean? Why was it important for him to use that language and how did he apply that point to the Philippians? What was happening in the church at Philippi? Such is the task of exegesis.

In the last two hundred years, and particularly in the last century, this kind of Bible reading has dominated the Christian world. It is, in part, the product of the Enlightenment. It has its value—it helps us understand the historical meaning of the text. But it also has its demerits—it often fails to recontextualize the text's meaning for the contemporary church and restricts the meaning of the text to what is discernible by historical-critical methods. The scholar has her role within the church as one who exegetes the text in ways that are beyond the knowledge and expertise of most, but the scholar does not exhaust the meaning of Scripture for the church. Every believer reads Scripture and the church as a community reads Scripture in such a way that God illuminates the church's way into the future. The church values her scholars, but she does not limit God's illuminating work to them alone.

The danger of exegetical study is the tendency to reduce Bible reading to historical pieces of data. It produces information. This is necessary, but insufficient. It is not enough to know facts or process information. Rather, Bible reading must seek God and commune with his presence. Consequently, a third way of reading is as important as the first two.

Silence

In addition to a "critical" reading of the Bible, Campbell encouraged a "devotional or sanctifying reading." Through this "means" disciples experience "communion with the Father, and with his Son," in a way that "is not vouchsafed to mortals in any other way."[31] This kind of reading is reflective or contemplative as individuals or communities sit in the presence of God.

There are many methods and resources for contemplative Bible reading.[32] We have suggested a few at the end of the chapter. But one of the most classic and ancient is the Benedictine method of *lectio divina* (divine reading). It is a simple but profound approach to meditating on the word of God. It can be practiced individually or communally (in small groups, Bible classes or even in the assembly). It has four steps.

The first step is *lectio* (reading). Select a verse or small paragraph of Scripture. Read the text over and over; not just twice or three times, but ten times or more. Read it silently and aloud—read it with your inner voice, but also vocalize it. Read it with different intonations and experiment with different emphases and inflections. Repetition is critically important. Do not rush over the text. Savor it. As Harding would say, "taste and see that the Lord is good" by meditating on his word (Ps 34:8). But in a spirit of silence, read with a listening ear and heart. Listen to the text.

The second step is *meditatio* (meditation). What is God saying to you? What is the connection to your daily life? Is God calling for a response? Mull over the text, and internalize the words. What phrases stand out from the constant repetition? Do any take hold of your heart? Do any impress you with the confluence of your life and the text? This is where we ponder the text. We engage the text with our feelings, reactions, associations, and challenges. Meditation is not about what the text meant, but how God is encountering us in the present.

The third step is *oratio* (prayer). Whatever thoughts came to you in reading the text, offer these to God. This is not a time of petition but another way of listening in dialogue with God. Turn your meditation from dialogue with yourself to dialogue with God. Share with God your reflections—how you are thinking and what you are feeling. Listen for God's response to your prayer. Embrace his promises in the word, and commit yourself to living out that word in your life. Invoke God to make it so in your life. Express your doubts, but take God at his word. Seek to trust him and pursue that trust in prayerful words.

The fourth step is *contemplatio* (contemplation). Be silent before God and quiet your soul. Rest in his presence. Let go of your mental activity. Practice the presence of God through silence, clearing your mind and trusting in the divine love. Allow a word or phrase from the text to fill your mind—one that has surfaced in the previous three steps. Repeat this word or phrase over and over; let it fill your mind. Let this be the word that guides you for the day and sustains God's presence in your life.

St. John of the Cross summarized the *lectio divina* in a paraphrase of Luke 11:9: "Seek in *reading* and you will find in *meditation*; knock in *prayer* and it will be opened for you in *contemplation*." Or, as Harding put it, "Read it; delight in it; meditate on it, memorizing striking passages, read them over and over and over again."[33] Learning to experience God through Scripture by reading it, meditating on it, praying it and contemplating God in its light will open the doors of our hearts. It is where we may seek God and find him. Finding him, we experience the transforming power of his presence.

CONCLUSION

Harding read Scripture as a divine drama where God redeems his creation through unfolding stages of history. Bible reading is the way we enter into the drama in order to understand our place in the story so that we may fully participate in the present reality of God's kingdom.

Many are using an increasingly popular analogy to locate our place in God's story.[34] It usually runs something like this. Living the story of God is like performing a drama. Our life in Christ is analogous to a group of Shakespearean disciples who want to perform a newly discovered six-act play by Shakespeare. But the fifth act is missing. We only have the first four acts and the last one. Suppose, however, these disciples wanted to perform this play. How can they perform it without the fifth act? They will have to improvise. In order to do so, they would have to "live and breathe" the works of Shakespeare. By knowing the mind of Shakespeare and thoroughly understanding the extant acts, they are able to improvise the fifth act in a way that is faithful to the other acts.

Christian discipleship is like performing the fifth act. Scripture bears witness to the mind of God in Christ. We have the first act—

Creation—and thus know God's intent for his world. We have the second act—Israel—and thus know how God intended his people to be a light to the Gentiles. We have the third act—Christ—and thus we see how the Son exegeted the Father (cf. John 1:18). We have the fourth act—the early Church—and thus know how the church in the New Testament lived and communally practiced the values of God in their time. And we know the sixth act—the new heaven and new earth—and thus know God's goal for his people. We are the fifth act and we currently perform that act best as we imaginatively enter into the mind of God in Christ. We seek to perform the fifth act in a way that is faithful to Scripture and faithful to how God has progressively worked in history to establish his kingdom.

But our ability to improvise and perform the fifth act depends directly on how well we know the other acts and attend to the work of the Spirit in interpreting those acts. Bible reading, both as individuals and as communities of faith, is foundational for performing the fifth act. In this sense, perhaps Harding is correct—"the most important thing in the world is daily, diligent, prayerful study of the divine word."[35]

DISCUSSION QUESTIONS

1. What has been your habit of daily Bible reading? What has helped or hindered you in your attempts to read daily?

2. What benefits have you experienced when you are constantly exposed to Scripture? What are the specific benefits for the three modes of listening to God?.

3. Which form of Bible reading is most transforming for you—story, study or silence?

CHALLENGE

Develop a daily habit of reading the Bible as a narrative story.

Find one hour a week where you can study a particular text in some depth.

Find fifteen minutes a day to meditate on a specific text in your daily reading.

Encourage your church to give more attention to the public reading of Scripture.

Join a small group bible study in order to listen to God in a communal way.

PRAYER

Our Father, we approach you through your Word, and thank you for providing your word as a guide for our lives. We are grateful for the story you have given us. Move in our hearts by the power of your Spirit that we might know you better. We seek your Word through your word. Give us the wisdom to understand and perform your word before the world that they might know you as we know you.

SUGGESTED RESOURCES

Gordon Fee and Douglas Stuart, *How to Read the Bible for All Its Worth*, 3rd ed. (Grand Rapids: Zondervan, 2003)

Richard Peace, *Contemplative Bible Reading: Experiencing God Through Scripture* (Colorado Springs: NavPress, 1998)

Susan A. Muto, *A Practical Guide to Spiritual Reading* (Pittsburgh: Epiphany Association, 1994)

Norvene Vest, *Gathered in the Word: Praying the Scripture in Small Groups* (Nashville: Upper Room, 1997)

Michael Casey, *Sacred Reading: The Ancient Art of* Lectio Divina (Liguour, MO: Triumph Books, 1995)

N. T. Wright, *The Last Word: Beyond the Bible Wars to a New Understanding of the Authority of Scripture* (San Francisco: HarperSanFrancisco, 2005)

Gary Holloway and Earl Lavender, *A Meditative Commentary on the New Testament* (Siloam Springs, AR: Leafwood Publishers, 2005-), multiple volumes.

SIX

RELEASING THE OPPRESSED: FELLOWSHIP AS A MEANS OF GRACE

Send bread now, brethren, and afterward the Bibles and preachers.
—David Lipscomb (1867)[1]

The poor of this world were the chosen vessels of mercy, the especially honored and blessed of God. They, as a class, constitute his elect.
—David Lipscomb (1869)[2]

Do you not know that the poor and lowly have more right in God's church than the rich…this is another peculiarity of the kingdom of Christ, which is not at all calculated to raise it in the estimation of the world.
—R. H. Boll (1899)[3]

America's Reconstruction and the Gilded Age (1865-1900) were wracked with contradiction. The South lay in ruins while urbanization and immigration swelled Northern cities. The promises of civil rights for African-Americans were exchanged for partisan political conquest.[4] This period saw the rise of extreme wealth concentrated in "robber barons" like the Rockefellers and Vanderbilts while pervasive poverty crossed all racial lines.[5] The separation between the haves and have nots, the powerful and the weak, was stark. Evidence for the vast divide is seen in the number of lynchings, riots, labor strikes and the emergence of the Populist Protest.[6]

Church leaders viewed these developments with suspicion. Some concluded that the church and her ministers were nothing more than "apologists and defenders of the wrongs committed against the... people simply because the perpetrators are possessors of wealth."[7] Cities, and especially their poor, frightened a good number of preachers. One Ohio preacher wrote that cities are moral deserts because they "contain the *dangerous classes*."[8] These included the illiterate non-Anglo-Saxon immigrant as a threat to law and order.

The founders of the NBST, living in the shadow of the second coming, advocated a countercultural perspective toward the dispossessed. Lipscomb responded vigorously to a contributor who mirrored this larger cultural prejudice against the poor. A writer in the *Apostolic Times* argued that churches need not expend energy on the destitute of the city because "they are about the only class" of people for whom "the gospel does but little good."[9] The editor of the *Gospel Advocate* could not believe what he was reading. He replied that "Christ came to save sinners, the worst, lowest, most depraved of sinners." Whether the poor were in Jerusalem, Antioch, Corinth, or Rome, the apostles followed the Savior's example by ministry to the oppressed. The *Apostolic Times* needed to rethink its theology in light of the kingdom. Rather than overlooking the poor, Lipscomb argues, "the poor possess preemptive rights in the kingdom of God."[10]

Lipscomb's unnamed correspondent was not persuaded. He reaffirmed his previous position. "We still hold, that the extremely poor of the great cities...besotted by vices of the all the baser sorts...are about the only class...among whom the gospel does but little good." In response, Lipscomb grounded his vision of the church's mission in the mission of Jesus.

> He showed his mission was to the wicked poor when he went to sinners, the outcasts, and ate with them. He received her with seven devils and cast them out. The poor adulteress was

> not spurned by him, a kindly word of sympathy was spoken, her self righteous accusers were condemned....To teach that certain classes are so degraded that the Gospel of God's love cannot reach them, is certainly to despise them, and is nigh akin to oppressing them.[11]

LIPSCOMB'S CALL FOR SACRIFICIAL FELLOWSHIP

The editorial duels with the *Apostolic Times* of 1873 were hardly idle talk. Lipscomb had by this time established himself as spokesperson for the oppressed.[12] Having passed through the barbarism of the Civil War, Lipscomb led a massive relief effort for the dispossessed of the South, ultimately securing over one hundred thousand dollars for the poor.[13] "Without timely aid," Lipscomb writes, "the masses, unable to raise crops," will perish.[14] Exacerbating the already desperate situation, a Cholera epidemic struck Nashville in 1866 and 1873 leading to the deaths of hundreds.

Poverty was no theoretical discussion for David Lipscomb. He experienced the hell of war along with thousands of others. He found himself in conditions approaching "actual starvation."[15] He writes of the anguish he felt as "every mouth full of food we ate was taken from women and children" who may have gone without. Epitomizing the plight of the poor was N. W. Smith, an evangelist from Georgia. Smith, in a report to the *Advocate*, relates how his family had been caught in the path of both Confederate and Union armies, with the result that all his worldly goods had been totally destroyed. He confessed he had been reduced to "beggary."[16]

Lipscomb's response to oppression was a radical call to fellowship. Attitudes like those in the *Apostolic Times* betrayed a failure to grasp the fullness of the gospel message. Fellowship was not, Lipscomb insisted, "agreement in theories or tenets of religion." If fellowship were to be defined by mere intellectual agreement between parties, he declares even "the demons and spirits of the wicked in hell have just as much fellowship as this." Rather biblical fellowship was a mutual love of brother for brother and sister for sister. Fellowship was a sharing and "aiding one another with their substance and by deeds of good service to those in need."[17]

Thus Lipscomb called upon Christians, especially in the North, to demonstrate true fellowship with those in the South. God in his providence, Lipscomb believed, had not only opened up a way for healing his church brutalized by war but also an opportunity to do incredible work in the name of Jesus. "We confidently aver that this generation has never seen…such a providential opening for preaching the Gospel as the Southern country presents at the present."[18] If Christians who had the resources fellowshipped with those who did not, God could effect a revolution. Many Christians simply wanted to ship Bibles South, but Lipscomb insists that other needs should take precedence.

> As highly as we appreciate the Bible, and its necessity to the temporal and spiritual well-being of man, a loaf of bread today, in the name of Christ, would do more in opening the hearts of our Southern people…than any number of Bibles, tracts or preachers. Send bread now, brethren, and afterward the Bibles and preachers.[19]

Unfortunately many Christians with resources fled the impoverished areas and left the dispossessed to fend for themselves. In June of 1873 nearly four hundred people in Nashville died from cholera. By the end of the summer over one thousand people would perish. Those especially hit hard were poor African-Americans. Some of Lipscomb's strongest language is found in articles reflecting on the trauma of this epidemic. "Every individual, white or black, that dies from neglect and want of proper food and nursing," he writes, "is a reproach to the professors of the Christian religion."[20]

Lipscomb could have withdrawn to his home outside the city and protected himself. But he personally entered the homes of the poor, nursing them, bathing them, and feeding them. Lipscomb praised the "Sisterhoods of the Romish church," who bravely performed acts of Christian ministry to relieve the sick. While differing widely on "tenants of religion," Lipscomb personally drove these angels of mercy in his buggy. The Episcopal pastor, Mr. Royce of Trinity Episcopal Church, likewise earned the admiration of the *Advocate* editor for his fellowship with the poor.[21] Lipscomb experienced his ultimate identification with the poor himself when he too contracted cholera.[22]

For Lipscomb the example of Jesus' self-denial was a call for Christians to share with him that emptying of self for others. Jesus is present in the poor. Anchoring his theology in Matthew 25 Lipscomb wrote:

> Christ is personified in his poor, helpless brethren, Matt. xxv: 40. In them, Christ appeals for help to himself. Who realizes this? . . . Let us realize that every helpless, needy one of our brethren is the personification of Christ to us appealing for help. He is our Christ, to be kindly welcomed and generously treated. Shall we cast our Christ from our doors and let him become a beggar from others….Inasmuch as you have done it unto one of the least of these my brethren, ye have done it unto me.'[23]

Directly linking the mission of the church to the ministry of Jesus, Lipscomb once again identifies Jesus with the poor in a radical way.

> This is the work for which the church was established….The church must be educated to the true appreciation of its proper work and solemn obligation that rests upon it to perform that work…Jesus Christ personified himself in his poor brethren. He stands to-day personified in the gaunt and hollow face, sunken eye, and half-clad emaciated form of widowed mothers and of hungry, starving children.[24]

Christians reproduce the life of Christ in their own. "The reproduction in our lives of the life of Christ is the end before us."[25] Our unity or fellowship with Christ finds expression in our doing the same work Jesus did. As Jesus gave up the glory of heaven so we must sacrifice our luxuries, wealth and pride to relieve the oppressed in this age.

> Just as Christ sacrificed his honors, glories, joys and possessions in heaven, to help poor helpless, fallen man on earth. This was the fellowship of God to man. I will give of my honors and joys to you, and take of your weaknesses, sufferings, and sorrows to myself, is the language of Jesus to man, in his mission to earth. Our fellowship for one another must be of this character....The man that can spend money in extending his already broad acres, while his brother and his brother's children cry for bread—the woman that can spend money in purchasing a stylish bonnet...merely to appear fashionable, while her sister...[is] shivering with cold...are no Christians... notwithstanding they have been baptized for the remission of sins.[26]

True fellowship, defined as sharing with the poor, functions as a means of grace in the NBST because it mediates the presence of Christ. We experience fellowship with Jesus as we share in his work. We also fellowship with the Servant of the Lord when we serve the poor, for he is mysteriously among the oppressed.

Lipscomb's concern for the oppressed was not limited to only poor white southerners. The NBST walked against the cultural grain regarding another dispossessed segment of society, African-Americans. Race, as it remains today, was a controversial topic. His family wrestled with the issue of slavery and decided to travel to Illinois while he was a child to free their slaves. This journey to freedom would cost Lipscomb his mother, two sisters and a brother.[27] However, upon their return to Tennessee the Lipscombs once again secured slaves. In fact, David Lipscomb owned five slaves according to the 1860 census just prior to the beginning of the Civil War—perhaps as a result of inheritance from his father.[28] The war itself may have given him a new perspective. Years later, near the close of the nineteenth century, he would reflect back on the institution of slavery and declare that "slavery was wrong." He believed that responsibility for the institution of slavery lay with previous generations who passed it on to his. He further believed that the North was just as responsible as the South for the "sin of instituting slavery in this country."[29] While it is true that Lipscomb mirrored many of the prevailing ideas of the day, he also transcended the racist culture in which he lived in profound ways.

In the winter of 1878 a notice appeared in the *Christian Preacher* that drew Lipscomb's attention. It reported that a "colored man" had presented himself to the congregation in McKinney, Texas for membership, raising protests from the white members. Lipscomb was concerned about this negative trend. Churches are rebelliously setting aside God's laws in favor of their prejudice. The world was full of race prejudice in the days of Jesus and the apostles too. The Jews hated the Samaritans and Gentiles hated Jews. But it was the mission of Christ to "break down middle walls, family prejudices, natural animosities, race antipathies and to unite all…tribes into one undivided and indivisible brotherhood."[30] Neither Christ nor the Holy Spirit tolerated those who objected to different races in the family of God, so neither should we. Lipscomb felt so strongly about this that he believed "it sinful to have two congregations in the same community for persons of separate and distinct races now." The very purpose of the church is to minister to the oppressed and for a church to act any other way is "criminal."[31]

Late in his career Lipscomb was embroiled in another controversy regarding African-Americans. A young African-American girl was brought to worship at the Bellwood Church. S. E. Harris protested that her presence was a great disturbance and requested that she be taken elsewhere. David Lipscomb was asked to resolve the conflict. Rather than exonerate the Bellwood Church, Lipscomb said:

> Christians of every different nation, tribe, country, of every social or political position, have equal privileges and rights in the service of God. No one as a Christian or in the service of God has the right to say to another 'Thou shalt Not,' because

> he is of a different family, race, social or political station.[32]

Not every reader appreciated Lipscomb's rebuke. One Texas reader discontinued his subscription to the *Advocate* with the words, "I am very old and feeble and do not wish to be insulted by your black Republican politics."[33]

The testimony that seals the identity of Jesus, according to Lipscomb, was simply that the "poor have the gospel preached to them."[34] What seals the identity of the church with God's kingdom is that it likewise fellowships the oppressed. This fellowship is not limited only to the Christian poor but to all the poor. Some contended that Christian relief work should be limited only to disciples. But for Lipscomb such an idea "never came from Christ"; Christ did not confine his mercy to his followers but showed it to all.[35]

Releasing the oppressed, setting the captives free, proclaiming the year of Jubilee was essential to the Christian walk in the NBST. Through fellowship with the poor we become partners in the ministry of Christ. We become more like Christ through emptying ourselves. We also share in a mystical communion with him because he is somehow present and identified with the oppressed.

RELEASING THE OPPRESSED IN GOD'S STORY

Redeemed refugees should make good neighbors. This is the point of the vast teaching in the Bible on justice towards the oppressed. As noted in chapter two, God's people are often characterized as aliens in their world. Near the beginning of the story God's people were literal slaves, literally without rights, literally without justice. There arose a Pharaoh who oppressed them and suppressed their growing presence in Egypt. These outcasts lived in perpetual fear. The oppressor brutalized them through a reign of terror aiming at the destruction of Israelite children. This tyranny became the context of Israel's salvation:

> So they put slave masters over them to oppress them with forced labor….They made their lives bitter with hard labor…

> in all their hard labor the Egyptians used them ruthlessly…. The Israelites groaned in their slavery and cried out, and their cry for help went up to God. God heard their groaning….So God looked on the Israelites and was concerned about them….Then the Lord said, 'I have indeed seen the misery of my people in Egypt. I have heard them crying out because of their slave drivers….So I have come down to rescue them….Then the Lord said to Moses, "Go tell Pharaoh and say to him, 'This is what the Lord says: Let my people go.'" (Ex 1:11-13; 2:23-25; 3:7-8; 8:1, NIV)

God redeemed slaves. God was moved by the cry of the powerless. This marvelous act of redemption by God is the basis of Israel's own way of life as God's people. They were redeemed slaves. They had experienced the euphoria of deliverance from a life of bondage. A people redeemed share redemption with other slaves.

Israel would never forget the gospel of the Exodus.[36] The book of Deuteronomy has the Exodus woven through its teaching. Deuteronomy bears witness to the great story (the Exodus), the great commandment (love God with our very being), and the great society (loving our neighbors). The Ten Commandments are rooted in the grace of God (Deut 5:6), especially the Sabbath commandment. Sabbath rest was granted to sons, daughters, servants, even animals because "you were slaves in Egypt and the Lord your God brought you out with a mighty hand" (Deut 5:15).

In reminding Israel of what it means to be the people of God, he states that they were a people of circumcised hearts (Deut 10:16) and defenders of the aliens (Deut 10:18). Moses first reminds them of the uniqueness of Yahweh: "He defends the cause of the fatherless and the widow, and loves the alien, giving him food and clothing." The people of God must follow God's own example. So Moses, after declaring God's own priority, commands: "And you are to love those who are aliens, for you yourselves were aliens in Egypt" (Deut 10:18-19). Israel, the rescued alien, was God's instrument in caring for other aliens.

The Psalmists impress upon the minds of Israelites the place the poor have in the heart of Yahweh through their liturgy. The following sampling represents an aspect of God's worship that is, perhaps, missing in our contemporary assemblies.

Rise up, O LORD; O God, lift up your hand;
    do not forget the oppressed . . .
But you do see! Indeed you note trouble and grief,
    that you may take it into your hands;
The helpless commit themselves to you;
    you have been the helper of the orphan . . .
O LORD, you will hear the desire of the meek;
    you will strengthen their heart,
You will incline your ear to do justice
    for the orphan and the oppressed,
    so that those from earth may strike terror no more.
    (Ps 10:12-18)

Father of orphans, defender of widows,
    such is God in his holy dwelling;
God gives the lonely a permanent home,
    makes prisoners happy by setting them free
    (Ps 68:5-6, Jerusalem Bible)

May he judge your people with righteousness,
    and your poor with justice.
May the mountains yield prosperity for the people,
    and the hills, in righteousness.
May he defend the cause of the poor of the people,
    and give deliverance to the needy,
    and crush the oppressor . . .
For he delivers the needy when they call,
    the poor and those who have no helper.
He has pity on the weak and the needy,
    and saves the lives of the needy.

From oppression and violence he redeems their life;
and precious is their blood in his sight.
(Ps 72:2-4; 12-14)

He upholds the cause of the oppressed
and gives food to the hungry.
The Lord sets prisoners free,
the Lord gives sight to the blind,
The Lord lifts up those who are bowed down,
the Lord loves the righteous.
The Lord watches over the alien
and sustains the fatherless and the widow . . .
The Lord reigns forever....
(Ps 146:7-10, NIV)

The prophets are laced with protests against religion that has a form of godliness but denies its power (2 Tim 3:5). Amos preached to a religious Israel, which was meticulous in her technical obedience to the forms of religion. Yet that society allowed seizure of the poor's land (Amos 2:7; cf. Micah 2:2), debt slavery (Amos 2:6), abuse of the courts in favor of the powerful (Amos 5:10, 15), sexual abuse of women (Amos 2:7b), and exploitation of the working poor (Amos 8:4-6).

The prophet Jeremiah, like Moses before him, forces Israel to ask what it means to be the people of God. Does having the temple and the altar make us his people? Does having a hill called Zion? Jeremiah says these are misplaced anchors of identity. Jeremiah declares that to know God, to be God's people, is nothing less than to live by God's values. Redeemed refugees, who know God, love other refugees. In a powerful oracle Jeremiah weeps for God's wayward people:

Woe to him who builds his palace by unrighteousness,
his upper rooms by injustice,
Making his countrymen work for nothing,
not paying them for their labor.
He says, 'I will build myself a great palace

with spacious upper rooms.'
So he makes large windows in it,
panels it with cedar and decorates it in red.
Does it make you a king to have more and more cedar?
Did not your father have food and drink?
he did what was right and just,
so all went well with him.
He defended the cause of the poor and needy,
and so all went well.
Is this not what it means to know me?'
declares the Lord. (Jer 22:13-16, NIV)

The Gospels paint the ministry of Jesus in complete harmony with this emphasis on justice in the Old Testament. Yahweh heard the cry of the oppressed and acted to save Israel. Jesus claims that language to describe his own ministry. Quoting from Isaiah 61, Jesus says,

The Spirit of the Lord is upon me,
because he has anointed me to bring good news to the poor.
He has sent me to proclaim release to the captives
and recovery of sight to the blind,
to let the oppressed go free,
to proclaim the year of the Lord's favor. (Luke 4:18-19)

The mission of Jesus was to release the oppressed. His mission is the same as Yahweh's in the Old Testament. Luke stresses throughout his Gospel the connection between the year of Jubilee and Jesus.[37] One of the many ways Luke does this is through his use of the word "save." Many modern Christians understand "salvation" in a wholly other worldly sense. Salvation is the forgiveness of sin and going to heaven. While this is one dimension of salvation it is by no means the whole. This truncated doctrine relegates ministry to the poor and oppressed as matters of secondary importance. But the ministry of Jesus, as well as the Law and the Prophets, calls that conclusion into question. Fully one fourth of the uses of the word "save" in the Gospels describe Jesus' miracles. Examples of those "saved" include blind Bartimaeus (Mark 10:52) and the man with the withered hand (Mark 3:4-5). Luke uses "salvation" to describe the healing of the centurion's servant (7:3), the sinful woman (7:50), the restoration of the demoniac (8:36), and the resurrection of a dead girl (8:50).

Jesus' encounter with Zacchaeus shows Luke's wider emphasis. Luke 19 tells the story of a zealous tax collector. He had piled up riches through corrupt taxation in which the Roman land lords allowed local subcontractors to collect more taxes than they passed onto Rome. Yet when Zacchaeus encountered Jesus, he was radically changed. He returned four times the amount he had taken through corrupt means. Then he gave half of his goods to the poor. Luke caps the story off with Jesus' words, "Today *salvation* has come to this house" (19:9). Salvation is understood squarely against the backdrop of Jubilee. Through healing the sick, feeding the poor, and releasing the oppressed, Jesus proclaims the good news. It is not merely his words, but his deeds that declare the good news of the kingdom. Luke describes salvation as new life, wholeness, forgiveness and healing.[38]

Jesus followed his Father's example in releasing the oppressed. He also called the people of God, as Moses did before him, to care for the powerless, the hungry, and dispossessed. The parable of the Sheep and the Goats (Matt 25:31-46) is no afterthought for Jesus. This parable reveals God's concern for the oppressed, Jesus' identification with the poor, and that our fellowship with the poor is ministry to Christ himself. Matthew 25 reinforces Jesus' claim that "justice, mercy and faithfulness" are in fact the "weightier matters of the law" (Matt 23:23).

A Model of Releasing the Oppressed

David Lipscomb believed that unsound doctrine could have a negative impact on the church's mission as an advocate for the oppressed. A mistaken understanding of Christ's mission leads to a mistaken view of Christianity. Lipscomb did not define Christ's mission as primarily an atonement for the removal of sin.

> The object of God's dealing with man, and especially the mission of Christ to earth, was to rescue the world from the rule and dominion of the evil one, from the ruin into which it had fallen through sin, and to rehabilitate it with the dignity and the glory it had when it came from the hand of God; to restore man—spiritually, mentally and physically—to the likeness of his maker.[39]

Mistaking the mission of God in Christ led some to conclude that the benefits of Christianity are primarily for the hereafter. But Lipscomb said the Christian religion is just as much intended to bless us here as in the afterlife.[40]

Others mistook the primary mission of the church as evangelism. This is certainly a high priority but not the first and highest object of the church. Rather, the goal of the local church is the perfecting of the saints. The second task, according to the *Advocate* editor, was fellowship with the poor.

> [T]he relieving of the physical ills that afflict humanity—feeding the poor, nursing the sick, caring for the orphan, visiting those that are in prison, and exhibiting a tender sympathy for the bodily ills, sorrows, misfortunes and afflictions of our fellow-creatures. This in the pure days of the Christian religion, was the work of the ministry.[41]

Sometimes Christians, Lipscomb believed, failed to be God's instruments of redemption in the world because of prejudice. That the people of God too often reflect attitudes of this age is painfully true. Rather than challenge injustice we, at times, boldly embrace the status quo. W. A. Cameron, a tireless evangelist in Florida, delivered a sermon to the Disston Ave. Church of Christ in Gulfport on August 15, 1954. He then preached the same sermon the next Sunday in Pinellas Park. There was demand for his lesson so he published it in booklet form. The date of the lesson is significant because it was delivered in the context of the *Brown v. Board of Education* Supreme Court case declaring an end to segregation. Cameron's sermon was called "*The ORIGIN and DEVELOPMENT of the NEGRO RACE*."[42] Cameron's blatant racism drips from the printed page. He is concerned that some "busy bodies" are trying to mess up "God's instruction" concerning blacks. He confesses that he has met one or two African-Americans who have done well in business. This must be accounted for by the "generous fertilization of white blood…but the genuine negro article is just what he has always been."[43] Perhaps Cameron is an extreme. But the fact that such preaching could be tolerated and even encouraged says something about how far the church drifted from the spirit of David Lipscomb.

Perhaps a model for preaching the gospel to the poor is Nashville's Central Church of Christ. This congregation was squarely in the NBST.[44] It was the brainchild of E. H. Ijams and A. M. Burton, who worried that the church was not fulfilling its mission toward the poor.[45] It defined its principal commitments in line with Lipscomb's emphasis as "seeking first the kingdom of God, thus worshipping God and serving man— REALLY SERVING 'in spirit and in truth.'"[46]

Ten months after Central opened its doors, A. M. Burton wrote a short report for J. N. Armstrong's *The Living Message*. The article, graced with eight photographs of ministry in action, describes the work of Central as:

> Striving to make peace and good will among men, in little things and in big things, working for peace and brotherhood between man and man; trying to do good to everybody: striving to develop the best in every man.[47]

Central offered free medical and dental care for the poor. The church provided educational and library services for the dispossessed. It offered classes in physical exercise, diet, hygiene, music, and the Bible. Central provided 45,000 hot meals from 1925 to 1928 to those who would have otherwise not eaten. The congregation purchased the Cumberland Hotel to provide housing for destitute women.[48]

Burton noted that many "wondered" how Central could have come up with such an outreach? "Our answer invariably is that we did not have to think it out. It is found in the Bible. Read Matt. 25:34-36."[49] Central did not ignore teaching people about Jesus and salvation as it relates to sin. Rather, Central preached the gospel in its wholeness to the whole person, and with astonishing results.

CONCLUSION

We are not called to be poor or oppressed. Rather God calls us to have a distinctive, gracious care, for the poor. John relates fellowship with God to caring for those in need: "How does God's love abide in anyone who has the world's goods and sees a brother or sister in need and yet refuses to help" (1 John 3:17). The oppressed poor, the alien without status, the homeless refugee, are to be accorded supreme dignity. They "as a class," Lipscomb reminds us, make up "God's elect." God's people, who are redeemed aliens, share in his ministry to the poor. We find fellowship with Jesus in this ministry as he works in and through us. We find fellowship with Jesus because he is present in the oppressed. Sharing with the poor is a means of grace in which the presence of Christ is mediated to us, transforming us into the image of the Son.

DISCUSSION QUESTIONS

1. What most surprises you about the NBST emphasis on releasing the oppressed? Why?

2. Is the doctrine of salvation broader than forgiveness of sins? How should this shape the mission of the church and in what the church invests its time, energy and money?

3. How does Lipscomb's exchange with the *Apostolic Times* reflect contemporary attitudes? What are our prejudices toward the poor?

4. What congregational activities are often characterized as fellowship that by their expense exclude the poor?

5. How does God view the poor? How do you?

CHALLENGE

Develop a habit of including the Biblical literature on justice in reading.

As a family get involved in an inner city rescue mission.

Increase your giving to the poor by ten percent.

PRAYER

Abba, Father, grant us grace to see your holy presence among the oppressed of our world. In the face of the homeless may we see Jesus. May we discern you in the inner city. Forgive us Father for forgetting our own redeemed state. We beg your power through the Holy Spirit to love as you have loved, to sacrifice as you have sacrificed. Amen.

RESOURCES

Jacqueline Jones, *The Dispossessed: America's Underclass from the Civil War to the Present* (New York: Basic Books, 1992)

Gary Holloway and John York, eds., *Unfinished Reconciliation: Justice, Racism & Churches of Christ* (Abilene: ACU Press, 2003)

Harold Shank, Anthony Wood, Ron Bergeron, *Up Close and Personal: Embracing the Poor* (Joplin, MO: College Press, 2000)

Ronald Sider, *Good News and Good Works: A Theology for the Whole Gospel* (Grand Rapids: Baker, 1999).

John G. Stackhouse, Jr. ed., *What Does It Mean to Be Saved? Broadening Evangelical Horizons of Salvation* (Grand Rapids: Baker, 2002)

Larry James, "Larry James Urban Daily," available at http://larryjamesurbandaily.blogspot.com/

SEVEN

COMMUNING WITH GOD: THE LORD'S DAY AND THE LORD'S TABLE

The Lord's Supper, however, is not a promise or a reward; but a means of grace until the promise is reached...The Lord's Supper is "the Lord's Table" indeed, because He ordained it; and there His disciples by faith hold "mystic, sweet communion" with their absent Lord, "in remembrance" of Him. But there is coming a bridal feast of love when they shall sit with Him, and He, with them, shall drink anew the fruit of the vine in the Father's kingdom. "Blessed are those who are invited to the wedding supper of the Lamb!" (Revelation 19:9.)

—Robert H. Boll (1948)[1]

The table of the Lord is a place where God provides sustenance and strength, warmth and vigor for his children. They should come to it as a precious privilege, and connect with this the full exercises provided in taking care of the needy, the afflicted, the suffering, the outcast ones of earth and a healthy, vigorous, joyous development of true spiritual life will be the result. Without this communing food and labor a weak and sickly development of life must be the result.

—David Lipscomb (1871)[2]

In 1881 James A. Harding had been conducting itinerant evangelistic meetings for five years. Early in that year he visited the Plum Street Church of Christ in Detroit, Michigan for the first time. He would spend two to three months with this church every year for the next eight years, sometimes twice a year.[3] Harding and Plum Street were completely infatuated with each other because they had such an agreeable common interest in the kingdom of God. His first article in the *Gospel Advocate* was about this church and he regarded it as a model.[4]

The congregation had its beginning in 1841, but permanently divided in 1867 after five tumultuous years. The root of the division was the "new interest" that Issac Errett represented when he was the "pastor" of the church for two years (1862-1864). The congregation divided over the progressive interests of those who supported missionary societies, introduced instrumental music into the assembly, and employed a "pastor system."[5] Sixty people began meeting at Fourth and Plum Street on July 26, 1868.[6] This represents one of the first of many sad episodes in the history of the Stone-Campbell Movement in the late nineteenth century as congregation after congregation divided along similar lines, including Harding's own home church in Winchester, Kentucky, in 1887.

By 1881, the church numbered 250 members and would grow to nearly 400 in the 1880s. They met three times on Sunday as well as for Wednesday "prayer meetings." The morning was reserved for the breaking of the bread, the afternoon for Sunday school and the evening was dedicated to evangelistic preaching. When the church gathered to break bread, they usually met for one and a half hours and the supper was "regarded as the prime object of the meeting" and its "principle feature." They practiced "mutual edification" where four or five men out of a group of twenty to thirty would exhort the church around the table rather than hiring a single preacher to instruct them. They took up a weekly collection dedicated to the poor, as well as a monthly collection for evangelism.[7]

Harding was impressed with its Sunday school and deemed it the equivalent of a "Bible College." The church was evangelistic. It began two outreach missions in the city in the 1880s and both of them developed into vibrant congregations by 1900. They supported international (Japan, Armenia) and domestic missions (helping itinerant evangelists). The Plum Street Church, according to Harding, was "not only a

Bible College, it [was] also a home and foreign missionary society." For Harding, it was everything "church" should be as an outpost of the kingdom.

THE DIVINE SERVICE

It has been said that Churches of Christ have three "sacraments:" baptism, the Lord's Supper and church attendance (Lord's day). This pithy remark embodies a significant aspect of the Stone-Campbell Movement. Alexander Campbell himself identified these three ordinances as the "positive institutions of the Christian system." They are the "indispensable provisions of remedial mercy" and "not one of them can be dispensed with any who desire the perfection of the Christian state and of the Christian character."[8] Their "remedial" significance is grounded in their relation to the "death, burial and resurrection of Christ" which is the "grounds of justification and hope."[9] In other words, they are gospel and "catholic" (universal) ordinances,[10] that is, "*means of grace*" through which "the hand of God" writes upon our hearts the character of his Son.[11] The Stone-Campbell Movement, from its very beginnings, has held that the gospel ordinances, or sacraments, are baptism, the Lord's Supper and the Lord's Day.

Theologically, these gospel ordinances have ordinarily (though with some variation) been construed in this manner: baptism as the means of grace for justification through the imitation of the death and resurrection of Jesus; the Lord's Supper as the means of grace for sanctification through remembrance and/or communion with the death of Christ; and the Lord's Day as the means of grace for communal worship through remembrance and/or celebration of the resurrection. In this sense, they are not only gospel ordinances, but also "sacramental" means through which believers experience the grace of the gospel in the Spirit. In other words, these gospel events mediate the presence of Christ to his community.

The Lord's Day "meeting, including all the services connected with it [Acts 2:42]," according to Lipscomb, is a divine "ordinance."[12] It was an appointed time and means by which believers serve God and are nourished by him. The Lord's Day is a day dedicated to the worship of God in which believers rest in his presence. The Sabbath command under the old covenant was rooted in the creation principle that both humanity and nature "needed one day of rest out of seven" and that day was "set apart" for the particular "service" of "worship."[13] While under the old covenant that day of rest was the seventh day, in the light of the resurrection of Jesus the new appointed day is the first day of the week since "every first day represents the resurrection day."[14] Indeed, according to Harding, just as "the seventh day was typical of the Sabbath rest that awaits the people of God, when for a thousand years they shall rest from sin, temptation, pain and sorrow; the first day of the week foreshadows the glorious beginning of a new life in the everlasting kingdom of God" upon "the new heaven and new earth."[15] Devoting the first day of the week exclusively to resting in the presence of God anticipates the eschatological rest of the people of God.

The first day of the week was the day on which believers gathered as a community to practice the spiritual disciplines of Acts 2:42. Lipscomb regarded Acts 2:42 as a description of "what was done at the worship on Lord's day."[16] At the center of this assemblage was the Lord's table. Lipscomb complained on several occasions that some churches only gathered when there was "a fine, flashy orator" available.[17] And Harding stressed "the importance of meeting on the Lord's day to 'break the loaf'" which was widely "neglected."[18] Apparently, some churches gathered to break bread only when a preacher was available.

Such neglect was not only an overestimation of preaching but also a devaluation of the significance of the Supper. For Lipscomb, the table was "a necessary arrangement to the Christian for perpetuating his spiritual life, and for developing his growth in grace and true holiness."[19] The Supper is necessary food for the soul—spiritual sustenance, divine help for human weakness.

> A man ought to partake of the Supper because he is a poor, weak, helpless being, needing help and strength from God.

> This ought to swallow up all other thoughts and purposes. Coming in this spirit, he will grow strong, be enabled to help his fellow-man, and honor God. To come in any other spirit than that of a needy suppliant for divine help is to fail at the essential point.[20]

The Supper was so central that Harding and Lipscomb believed the exclusive use of a single preacher for the breaking of the bread was detrimental to the spiritual health of the congregation. 1 Corinthians 11-14 demonstrates that a wide number of people participated in teaching the church.[21] Harding counseled that as many "as possible should take part in the services," including "three or four" making "short talks and others reading Scripture."[22] The Spruce Street Church in Nashville, for example, rarely had meetings where "fewer than four or five" edified the assembly.[23] The substitution of one preacher for mutual edification, Harding believed, was "one of the chief causes of the lack of spirituality" among the churches he visited.[24]

This emphasis on the Lord's Day, however, is balanced by an equally important stress on discipleship and living for the sake of the kingdom. Lipscomb describes the balance with the metaphor of "food and labor." The Lord's table is the food of believers, but their discipleship in the kingdom is their labor. "In the Lord's supper we find spiritual food," Lipscomb writes, and "in visiting the sick, feeding the hungry, clothing the naked, caring for the widow and the fatherless, we are doing spiritual work."[25] One cannot be separated from the other. The Lord's day and discipleship must complement each other. "We cannot live by food alone spiritually."[26] Ethics (discipleship) and assembly (Lord's day) are bound together.

LIFE AND ASSEMBLY

The dichotomy between life (discipleship) and assembly (communal liturgies) is unfortunate. They should be correlated rather than compartmentalized. We bring sacrificed lives as sacrificial offerings into the assembly and assembly empowers sacrificial living as God mediates his presence to us through communal praise. The assembly, with its table, is a means of grace. When assembly devalues discipleship so that one day a week becomes the essence of Christianity or when discipleship devalues assembly so that the Lord's day becomes merely a function of mutual encouragement, then both lose their power and purpose. We seek a balance that values the unique presence of God through the "sacrament" of assembly, while at the same time valuing how disciples of Jesus are daily instruments of kingdom presence in the world.

Sacrificial Living

Worship is much more than the corporate assembly. It is the submission and sacrifice of our lives for the purpose of glorifying God in everything we do. We offer our lives as a sacrifice before God in response to God's work for us. Perhaps the most significant text for this understanding is Romans 12:1-2:

> I appeal to you therefore, brothers and sisters, by the mercies of God, to present your bodies as a living sacrifice, holy and acceptable to God, which is your spiritual worship. Do not be conformed to this world, but be transformed by the renewing of your minds, so that you may discern what is the will of God—what is good and acceptable and perfect.

Paul parallels the Old Testament offering of a sacrificial animal—an act of worship—with the offering of our own bodies as a liturgical act. In response to what God has done, in view of his mercy, we offer ourselves—our bodies, the whole of our lives—to God as our worshipful response. We live transformed lives conformed to the will of God rather than the pattern of the world. As God's people, we are a "spiritual house, to be a holy priesthood, to offer spiritual sacrifices acceptable to God through Jesus Christ" (1 Pet 2:5).

Everything we say or do is offered as a sacrifice to God's glory. Paul extended the ritualistic sacrificial language of the Old Testament to include the whole of the believer's life. Ministry (e.g., benevolence), then, is as much worship as singing praises to God. Hebrews 13:15-16 describes both with sacrificial language: "Through Jesus, therefore, let us continually offer to God a sacrifice of praise—the fruit of lips that confess his name. And do not forget to do good and to share with others, for such sacrifices God is pleased."

There is no absolute difference between praising God with our lips and sharing our possessions with others. Both are worship. Whether we sing praises to God as part of a corporate assembly or buy a homeless person a meal, we are worshipping God. Whether we confess the name of Jesus through song in an assembly or help a widow pay her rent, we are worshipping God. Our life—whether in assembly or in the inner city—is our worship.

Sometimes this New Testament attitude is contrasted with the Old Testament. This is misleading. When Old Testament worshippers offered their sacrifices, they offered lambs, goats, doves or some other gift to God. These gifts were tokens and symbols of devoted lives. The Hebrew worshippers offered their worship through the gift of sacrifice as a symbol of their own dedication to God. The animal sacrifice symbolized the sacrifice of their own lives. Even in the Old Testament, all of life was worship.

For example, Psalm 40 reflects what God really wants when his worshippers come before him. The burnt offering is not what God ultimately desires. He wants what the burnt offering symbolizes—a life dedicated to his will (40:6-8):

> Sacrifice and offering you do not desire,
>   but you have given me an open ear.
> Burnt offerings and sin offerings
>   you have not required/
> Then I said, "Here I am:
>   in the scroll it is written of me.
> I delight to do your will, O my God;
>   your law is within my heart."

The important point about sacrifice is the life one brings before God. God values pierced ears more than the sacrifice. Pierced ears symbolized a life-long pledge on the part of a servant to a master (cf. Ex 21:6; Deut 15:17). In other words, God values a person's life-long service more than any particular burnt offering. God values a heart dedicated to doing the will of God. This is the worship God desires (cf. Mark 12:28-34).

Sacrificial Offerings

If all of life is worship, then so is the assembly. But worship is the focus of the corporate assembly of God's people in a unique sense. The people of God as a community gather to worship God. This dual sense of worship—one referring to all of life and the other referring to the assembly of God's people—is present in the Old Testament. Psalm 40:6-8, as noted above, teaches that our obedient life is a sacrifice to God's honor, but it also expects that God's people will gather to praise God (Ps 40:9-10).

> I told the glad news of deliverance in the great congregation;
> See, I have not restrained my lips, as you know, O Lord.
> I have not hidden your saving help within my heart,
> I have spoken of your faithfulness and salvation;
> I have not concealed your steadfast love and your faithfulness
> from the great congregation.

Psalm 40, and the Old Testament in general, holds the tension between "all of life is worship" and "the worship assembly" in wonderful balance. It is not an either/or dichotomy, but a both/and reality.

When Israel gathered as a "great assembly," they remembered the "day of assembly" (Deut 4:10; 9:10; 18:16, NIV)—the day Israel entered into covenant with God at Mount Sinai (Ex 19-24). On that day Israel became an assembly (church) of God (cf. Acts 7:38). In light of their covenant with God, Israel gathered regularly in "holy assemblies"(NIV). Leviticus 23 and Numbers 28-29 detail them, including the Sabbath, the Passover, the Feast of Weeks, the Feast of Trumpets, the Feast of Tabernacles and the Day of Atonement. Israel also gathered as an assembly at various special times or events, like the dedication of the Tabernacle (Ex 35:1), donations for the Temple (1 Chr 29:1,10,20), the dedication of the Temple (2 Chr 5:2,3; 6:3,12,18; 7:8) and at covenant renewals (2 Chr 29:23-32; 30:2,4,13,17,21-25; Neh 8:1,18). God created Israel as a people who would glorify him and commune with him. Indeed, Israel was destined to be an "assembly of peoples" (Gen 28:3; 35:11; 48:4; NIV) which all nations would eventually join. The prophets of Israel saw a day when all the nations would gather with Israel in Jerusalem to worship as a great assembly (cf. Isa 2:2-3; 30:3-5; Zech 14:16).

Worship assemblies, then, were integral to the life of Israel. The Psalms often presuppose a gathering of God's people. Indeed, we might envision the Psalter as the hymnbook of the assemblies of Israel (see Pss 22:22,25; 26:12; 35:18; 89:5; 107:32; 111:1) In these assemblies Israel entered the presence of God, or, as the Hebrew literally says, Israel went before the face of God (cf. Deut 26:10; 1 Sam 1:19; Ezek 46:3, 9; Ps 22:27; 86:9; 1 Chr 16:29; 20:18). We come before the face of God when we gather to worship him (Pss 95:2; 96:6,9,13; 98:6,9; 100:2).

Worship within the corporate assembly, then, is our response to the presence of God among his gathered people. God is present by grace, and his gathered people respond through faith when they offer their gifts of praise which flow from their lives of service. God is both the subject and the object of this worship. God as subject offers his presence to his people, dynamically engages them in communion, and enjoys the mutual giving. As the object of worship, the gathered assembly offers its gifts to the one who sits on the throne. They "go to church" to be part of God's assembly that goes before the face of God where God is present among his people.

Experiencing God in Communal Assembly

Church attendance, or gathering with the assembled people of God, is a sacrament—depending on how one defines sacrament. We do not mean the assembly is something magical or institutional. Rather, we mean that God mediates his presence to his people through their assembling together. We mean that as we gather together we are lifted up into the presence of God to surround his heavenly throne.

Drawing Near the Throne of God

The sermon the church has called "Hebrews" is addressed to a struggling community of believers. Some have already given up the habit of assembling with the community, some are drifting out of the community, some are regressing, and others are discouraged. The preacher speaks a word of encouragement (13:22).

The sermon assumes an assembled group of believers. It's language envisions the assembly "drawing near" to God, or approaching his throne, or entering into his presence in the context of this assembly (cf. Heb 4:16; 7:25; 10:22). Believers enter the presence of God as a gathered people. Certainly this is not the only time they enter that presence—we can "draw near" to God anywhere, anytime—but the assembled church is a moment of such entry through the curtain into the Holy of Holies.

Hebrews 10:19-25 is important for understanding the meaning of assembling. Through the blood of Christ we have access to the heavenly sanctuary of God's presence; we enter the Holy of Holies. Because we have this access to the heavenly sanctuary, (1) we draw near to God, (2) we hold fast our profession of faith; and (3) we keep on caring for one another as we assemble together regularly. To "draw near to God" (used also in Heb 4:16; 7:25; 10:1, 22; 11:6; 12:18, 22) is liturgical language. Its Old Testament meaning is to approach God in worship (such as at sacrifices and sacrificial meals; cf. Ex 12:48; 16:9; Lev 9:5-8; 21:17-23; Num 16:40; 18:3-4, 22; 1 Sam 14:36). We draw near to God just as the priests of the Old Testament did (Heb 10:1). We enter God's presence to worship him as we offer our gifts. We draw near in a covenantal relationship which was enacted when we had our hearts sprinkled with his blood and our bodies washed in water. To "draw near" to God is to enter into his presence. It is to come before the face of God as an assembly of God's people.

Eschatological Gathering of the People of God

The New Testament concept of "church" is partly rooted in the Old Testament idea of "assembly." Hebrews 12:18-21 reminds us that on Israel's "day of assembly" it gathered at Mount Sinai in the presence of God. Analogously, when the church gathers in assembly (Heb 10:22-25), it gathers in the presence of God. But the significance of the church's gathering is greater than Israel's. We come into the presence of God as his eschatological community (Heb 12:22-24):

> But you have come to Mount Zion and to the city of the living God, the heavenly Jerusalem, and to innumerable angels in festal gathering, and to the assembly of the firstborn who are enrolled in heaven, and to God the judge of all, to the spirits of the righteous made perfect, and to Jesus, the mediator of a new covenant, and to the sprinkled blood that speaks a better word than the blood of Abel.

When the people of God assemble, their gathering becomes holy ground. We draw near to God by entering his heavenly dwelling place through the blood of Jesus Christ where thousands of angels and the spirits of the faithful are gathered around the throne of God. So as saints around the world gather to worship God, we are all gathered at the same place, that is, we are assembled in the throne room of God. We are assembled on Mount Zion where his angels and saints serve him day and night. In our worship assemblies, as the song says, "We are standing on holy ground. And I know that there are angels all around."[27]

The preacher of Hebrews projects us into the throne room of God. We are in the Most Holy Place. We come—in our daily lives, but also in our assemblies—to Mt. Zion, the heavenly Jerusalem. We come to God who is surrounded by his angels and the saints who previously died and now enjoy God's presence (as in Rev 7:9-17; cf. 14:13). We are not alone! We gather with thousands of angels, millions of saints—both on earth and in heaven.

Eating at the King's Table

This eschatological horizon reminds us that the root metaphor of the Lord's Supper is neither tomb nor altar, but table. Through the Supper disciples experience the eschatological joy of the risen Christ as he hosts our communal meal.

The link between the Supper and the second coming of Christ is acknowledged by all in the light of 1 Corinthians 11:26 ("until he comes"). However this link is sometimes reduced to either a (1) temporal terminus (e.g., we eat the Supper till he comes and then there is no more Supper); (2) a promised fact (e.g., when we eat the Supper we acknowledge the fact that he will come again); or (3) a pledge of the future (e.g., when we eat the Supper we are again promised that Christ will return). In each of these, eschatology is wholly future. The spiritual dynamic of the Lord's Supper remains either memory, future anticipation and/or nourishment. There is no eschatological dynamic in the present but only an absent Christ whose return we await through memory and spiritual sustenance. Fundamentally, this lack of eschatological "alreadiness" engenders a solemn and funerary atmosphere that is more consistent with the metaphor of altar than table. If Jesus is wholly absent, then sorrow pervades the table. But if Jesus is already present in some sense, then we relish the communion with the living Christ.

When we reclaim the "alreadiness" of the eschaton, however, and understand that the risen Christ is present at the table with us, joy and thanksgiving envelope the table. It is a place where we experience the already/not yet tension—Jesus is absent, but he is present. The *eschaton* has "already" arrived in some sense; it is not a mere future anticipation. The eschaton has "burst" through the shadows; it is no mere anticipation of the future but a mysterious experience of it.

The biblical ground for this understanding of the Lord's Supper is the recognition that the Supper is as much about the resurrection of Jesus as it is his death. Jesus promised his disciples that he would eat and drink again with them in the kingdom of God. He ate with them in his ministry. He ate with them at the Last Supper. And he ate with them after his resurrection. The continuity between ministry meals (e.g., Luke 9), the Last Supper (Luke 22) and post-resurrection meals (Luke 24) is the presence of the living Christ in the breaking of the bread.

The solemnity and apparent sadness of our current experience of the Supper in the contemporary church does not fit the Emmaus road experience (Luke 24). Christians need to revision the Supper as an experience of resurrection joy at the kingdom table rather than as an altar of sacrifice. The Easter meals shaped the disciples' understanding of the Lord's Supper.

Just as the Emmaus narrative moves from the non-recognition of Jesus to the recognition of Jesus at the table, so the church recognizes Jesus at the table. There we recognize the victory of the resurrection as we eat and drink with Jesus in hope. At the table we bring all our "Fridays" to Jesus and celebrate the victory of Christ on Sunday. The table transforms "Friday" into "Sunday." Unfortunately, the church still generally practices the Supper as if it were still Friday rather than Sunday. But the point of the Supper is that we celebrate Sunday and experience the reality that God has overcome Friday. Sunday reinterprets and renews our Fridays. The mystery of the resurrection is present in the Eucharist.

The Lord's Supper is a continuation of the post-resurrection meals with his disciples but in a post-ascension situation. Our joy is already here though it is not yet fully realized.

The church should not abandon, of course, memorialism (remembrance) or a sense of mystical presence through the bread and wine. But these perspectives must be brought under the horizon of the *eschaton* which is the substance of the Christian faith. In the Eucharist we remember the future because the new (eschatological) human, Jesus the Messiah, is present at the table as an earnest of the future.

Eating with the Saints

When we visualize and experience the risen Christ at the table with us, a pleasant smile appears on our faces. The smile sometimes annoys those sitting around us in "church." But the smile is produced by the sense that we are already at the eschatological table with Jesus, and with Joshua, Dad, Sheila and with all the saints.[28]

The movie *Places in the Heart*, starring Danny Glover and Sally Field, dramatizes this point. During the movie several people die, but at the end they reappear in a communion service that is the movie's final scene. The camera pans the rows as each participant partakes and some of those who have already died are again on those pews drinking the communion cup. The scene portrays the eschatological reality that we now experience. As we eat and drink in the presence of God, we eat and drink with saints who have gone before us. As we gather around the table, the Spirit of God lifts us up into the throne room of God where we experience a foretaste of fellowship at the messianic table in the kingdom of God.

Given this vision of eschatological joy in festive assembly, the preacher of Hebrews exhorts his people to persevere in their faith because they already possess the goal, that is, they already experience eschatological joy through faith. That is our hope and that is why we continue the journey. Since we have already received the kingdom in some sense, let us worship and be grateful (Hebrews 12:28).

CONCLUSION

We believe discipleship is important, but we also believe that assembly is essential to the shaping of the people of God into the image of God. The assembly shapes communal identity and empowers discipleship.

The assembly of God's people means that we worship God, we confess our hope, and we encourage each other (Heb 10:22-25). Gathering in his presence anticipates a future assembly around the throne of God when God will fully dwell with his people in the new Jerusalem on the new heaven and the new earth (Rev 21:1-4). There we shall see the face of God and serve him day and night. Revelation 7 provides a picture of this eschatological gathering where "a great multitude that no one could count, from every nation, tribe, people and language" stands before the throne of God (7:9). This great multitude cried in a loud voice, "Salvation belongs to our God, who sits on the throne, and to the Lamb" (7:10). They have had their robes washed in the blood of the Lamb (7:14), and "they are before the throne of God and serve him day and night in his temple; and he who sits on the throne will spread his tent over them" (7:15).

When the people of God gather, we experience the presence of God. We remember the history of God's involvement with his people and we anticipate heaven's eschatological assembly. The people of God are encouraged by God's presence and they encourage each other. Worship has both a vertical (offered to God) and an horizontal (mutual encouragement) aspect. Both are a function of gathering. Indeed, we are mutually encouraged by being together in God's presence. That is why we "go to church."

DISCUSSION QUESTIONS

1. How is the Plum Street church like or unlike your congregation? In what ways might their example and the teaching of the NBST positively influence the life of your church?

2. What is the relationship between life and assembly? Instead of compartmentalizing these two dimensions of worship, how might we integrate them and see them as a whole?

3. How does the eschatological horizon of the Supper enrich and/or disturb your understanding and experience of Sunday assembly?

CHALLENGES

As you worship with your church this Sunday, envision the throne room of God and see the church universal gathered there with you. As you eat, envision sitting at the table not only with Jesus but with your departed loved ones.

Devote a Sunday wholly to God and his kingdom work—prioritize the kingdom over your interests, ballgames, and wants for one whole day. Consider it a day made "holy" to the Lord.

PRAYER

Father, Abba, thank you for the promise of your presence when we gather as your people. We seek your face and your strength. We glory in your presence, and we are humbled by the invitation to your table hosted by your Son. Lord God, all honor, power, and glory belong to your name and to your Son. Fill us with your Spirit that we might be people who walk in the world with the glow of your presence. Amen.

SUGGESTED READING

John Mark Hicks, *Come to the Table: Revisioning the Lord's Supper* (Orange, CA: New Leaf Books, 2002).

Peter Leithart, "The Way Things Really Ought to Be: Eucharist, Eschatology, and Culture," *Westminster Theological Journal* 59 (Fall 1997), 159-76.

John Zizioulas, *Being as Communion* (Crestwood, N.Y.: St. Vladimir's Seminary Press, 1985).

Alexander Schmemann, *The Eucharist* (Crestwood, N.Y.: St. Vladimir's Seminary Press, 1987).

Robert Richardson, *Communings in the Sanctuary*, ed. C. Leonard Allen (Orange, CA: New Leaf Books, 2001).

EIGHT

CRYING FOR THE KINGDOM: THE PRIVILEGE OF PRAYER

It is a good rule to pray regularly four times each day, morning, noon, evening, and night, and other times when occasion requires it.
—James A. Harding (1902)[1]

God is as ready to answer prayer as ever; it is easy for him to do it as it ever was; there is not a good thing that he is not willing, ready and able to give in answer to the prayer of faith; but it is more probable that prayers of faith are very scarce. Here is an enormous power, the mightiest that can be used by a mortal, that few of us use as we could and should.
—James A. Harding (1905)[2]

In 1910 the minister for the Pearl and Bryan Church in Dallas, Texas, accused James A. Harding of having a perverted mind. L. S. White determined that Harding "had his mind warped so long with this anti-scriptural, George Mueller theory of 'trusting God,' which is so foreign to the word of God, that it would be very hard for him to now either learn or teach the truth on this question."[3] Harding himself was not only poisoned but was now trying to foist upon the brotherhood "that little George Mueller theory." Mueller, a pastor among the Plymouth Brethren, simply advocated that disciples "look directly to God for support."[4]

According to Harding, Mueller was among God's elite. His faith "rank[s] in the same class with Abraham." Harding doubted "if he has been excelled in faith and in devotion to God by any man that has lived since the apostolic age."[5] Certainly Mueller, and Alexander Campbell, were "the two most remarkable men of the nineteenth century."[6]

Harding had been following and promoting Mueller's story for at least twenty years when White castigated him.[7] Mueller's crime was that he believed God would answer his prayers. Through prayer he had, Harding informed White, built five orphanages. Through prayer he had fed and clothed ten thousand orphans. Through prayer he had distributed millions of Bibles. Yet Mueller never asked for a dime. The money did not come from himself, for he lived poor and died poor. How could he do such work, Harding inquired? The loving God truly hears the prayers of his faithful child. Harding chided White that he did not know "the difference between theory and practice."[8] Mueller's was no theory in Harding's life but rather a demonstration of the faithfulness of God.

Prayer, and how God responds to prayer, lay at the heart of the Harding-White disagreement. Does God still answer prayer as he did in biblical days? Or does God answer prayer indirectly through laws he established to run the world smoothly? For Harding the shadow of the coming age sacralized the world as a sphere of divine action. White's deistic secularization expelled God from directly interfering in this age.

HARDING ON PRAYER

Prayer is the fourth "means of grace." These four means begin and end with communication with the Father. We begin by listening to our Father and end by talking with him. Harding bathed his life in prayer with God "morning, noon, evening and night."[9] Through prayer the power of God is unleashed in the service of the saints. Prayer is the cry for the kingdom by those living in the shadow of the second coming.[10] Prayer is a cry for God's will to be done on earth as it is in heaven.

Unlike some of his contemporaries, Harding embraced the mystery of prayer. "We do not understand the philosophy of prayer;"

Harding wrote, and "it is not necessary that we should."[11] In the face of the inexplicable the Christian response is faith.

Though mysterious, Harding believed prayer was rooted in some core truths that if not cherished would die on the vine. Perhaps most fundamental for Harding was faith in a certain kind of God. Though fully sharing the belief that God is a sovereign king, Harding insisted that disciples wrestle with what kind of king. The king of the universe was none other than a loving father.

> I believe that God loves his faithful children with a very great love. I believe he is near to them, takes great pleasure in them, knows their needs perfectly, and that he can supply their wants at any time, any where, under any circumstances. Indeed, I believe he loves these faithful children so much he guards them with a perfect care.[12]

Again Harding said "he is the gentlest and most loving, the most just and most merciful of all fathers."[13]

Because God is the most loving Father in the universe, he pays attention to his family living in this rebellious age. Through faith Christians cry to God as "a child to a father" believing he will "work in our affairs."

> We pray for food, for strength, for guidance, for deliverance from temptation, for extension of Christ's kingdom, for the welfare of our families, and so on; now if these prayers avail at all, in any way, in securing for us food, strength, guidance, and deliverance from temptation…it is because in answer to them there is put forth…a power incomprehensible to mortals.

Closely related to God as a loving Father was the bedrock belief that God is the same yesterday, today and tomorrow. A growing secular deism was destroying the church's faith in the dynamic God of the

Bible. Deists believed that God created the world through miracle but now only worked through natural law and human effort. Harding notes this infection of deism:

> Now a few people seem to be under the impression that all divine interventions have ceased since the death of the Apostles, and that since then there have been no super mundane or super-human influences known on earth. They think God gave the word and stopped—a very low and very erroneous conception of the reign of Christ….God has not changed in the least from all eternity. He is the same yesterday, to-day and forever. He has always loved and blessed those who love and serve him in trusting faith.[15]

Though Churches of Christ were growing because of God's work though many tireless evangelists, of whom Harding was one of the greatest, Harding believed there was inherent danger in some of their methods. Many were brought into the church through "high pressure protracted meetings" and had "very poor conceptions of what a Christian ought to be."[16] Preachers were neglecting instruction in prayer, daily Bible reading and the Lord's day. Critiquing these ministers, Harding suggested they found it easier to preach about "escaping hell and getting into heaven" in order to make their numbers look good than about the importance of leading kingdom lives.[17]

Church buildings were full but disciples full of faith were scarce. Indeed, what hindered a true evangelistic revolution, in Harding's view, was the lack of Bible reading and faith in the special providence of God responding to the cries for the kingdom in the churches.[18] Harding was so bold as to suggest this "pure infidelity"[19] did not start with the laity but with the leadership. Perhaps, he suggested, the most blighting curse on the kingdom was not societies or instrumental music, which were then dividing churches, but unbelief. Satan's best helpers, Harding dared to say, were those "honored by their fellows as ministers in the Church of God" but unbelievers in God's continuing action in response to the cries for the kingdom.[20]

Illustrating this trend, Harding shared an anecdote from the evangelistic trail. During one of his meetings, Harding met a brother before the service who told him he had been praying that he might "speak the oracles of God." Later that evening Harding thanked the man, testifying that God had answered his prayer.

> When I told him that I had been providentially led to speak what I did speak and to leave out some things which I had been accustomed to preach when discussing that subject, he was incredulous. He did not believe God had anything to do with my leaving out what had been omitted. He seemed to think that prayer was a form which should be complied with but we need not expect it to bring any blessing from God. Nor would it have brought but indignation and wrath, if none of us had believed any more than he did. We need not expect the prayer of doubt or of unbelief to be answered with a blessing.[21]

Since prayer is communication with God, Harding believed it is often best joined with Scripture. God communicates his presence to us through his word and the Christian responds to his gracious initiative. Scripture takes on renewed vitality when a "portion of the word of God" is read with "care and meditation before each prayer."[22] Through an "hour or more" of earnest communion with God through word and prayer, disciples find "a day's work for Christ already mapped out." Through continual exposure to God's presence, Christians "grow better" through transformation. Thus prayer changes not only the world[23] but disciples into the image of Jesus Christ.[24]

For what are disciples to pray? Harding believed that through prayer God allowed Christians to participate in the achievement of his divine purposes for the world. God is the "Great Weaver" who is weaving a masterpiece. Our prayers become the "wool that is woven into the eternal warp of his purpose."[25] Thus the goal of the kingdom should drive the prayers of Christians. R. H. Boll captured the heart of the

NBST on prayer when he prayed to be free from competing allegiances to the kingdom in whatever form they may be.

> O my Father, deliver me from the domination of money. My heart is deceitful above all things and desperately sick, only thou canst know the depth of it. Without realizing that it was so, I was on my way to become a professional. And now, Father, forgive thy penitent servant, and guide his wayward feet unto thy paths. Make me wholly free from the fear of man and the fear and love of money. Help thou mine unbelief! May I by thy grace love thee, even thee alone and supremely; and because I love thee may I love thy truth, and the souls of men. Enable me to lay all my burdens and concerns as to this world's affairs upon the God who will in no wise fail nor in any wise forsake them that rest their trust on him; and then go forth to do all thy will, even thine, unto the end.[26]

CRYING FOR THE KINGDOM IN GOD'S STORY

The biblical narrative is punctuated by God's people crying for the kingdom. Cain cried for mercy. Abraham interceded for Sodom. Jacob prayed all night. Moses pled for Israel. Hannah begged for a son. David cried for grace. Elijah prayed for victory over false gods. Habakkuk demanded justice. Nehemiah confessed the sins of God's people. Jesus prayed for believers. Peter asked God to raise the dead. Paul prayed that the Spirit of wisdom and revelation would be granted to Christians.

At the root of prayer is relationship. The prayer warriors of ancient Israel fervently believed that Yahweh had initiated a covenant of love (Deut 7:8-9; Ps. 136) and sustained them by his faithfulness (Ps 121; Ps 124). The God of Israel was not an impersonal force or a projection of the community or a natural phenomenon. Rather, Israel experienced a personal God on both a corporate and individual level through his mighty acts.

Because the Israelites believed God loved and kept her, a characteristic of Old Testament prayer is that it covers all aspects of life.

Adoration flows from the lips of the pious Israelite:

> Nevertheless I am continually with you;
>   you hold my hand.
> You guide me with your counsel,
>   and afterward you will receive me with honor.
> Whom have I in heaven but you?
>   and there is nothing on earth that
>   that I desire other than you. (Ps 73:23-25)

Israel's language of prayer included confession of both individual and corporate sin. Confession was essential for the deepening of the relationship:

> O LORD God of heaven, the great and awesome God, who keep covenant and steadfast love…let your ear be attentive and your eyes open to hear the prayer of your servant that I now pray before you day and night for your servants, the people of Israel, confessing the sins of the people of Israel, which we have sinned against you. Both I and my family have sinned. (Neh 1:5-6)

Experiencing God's healing and forgiveness was a way of life for Israel. Cries of thanksgiving flow from a community conscious of divine gifts:

> O give thanks to the LORD, call on his name,
> make known his deeds among the peoples. (1 Chronicles 16:8)

The God Israel thanked for meeting her needs is also the God she cried to when in need.

Unlike many modern westerners, the Old Testament sees humanity as a psychosomatic unity. Rather than dividing reality into "spiritual" and "physical," the Hebrews believed everything fell under the divine reign. Thus Israel made her supplications, or petitions, known to God

(1 Sam 1:17). "May the LORD grant all your requests" (Ps 20:5). The most mundane things invited God's attention and Israel prayed for them. The Hebrew of Hebrews prayed, "Give us today our daily bread" (Matt 6:11).

Prayer was the rhythm of life for the Old Testament saint.[27] The cadence of life begins with morning prayer (Ps 5:3; 119:147). Some pray morning, noon and evening (Ps 55:17; Dan 6:10). Indeed, the saint strives to pray without ceasing (Pss 72:15; 105:4).

The threads of prayer glow even brighter as we follow the story into the Gospels and church. Here we see part of the tapestry that God has been weaving from the prayers of Old Testament saints.

Luke, as in many other areas, consciously tells his version of the Gospel of Jesus against the backdrop of Israel's hopes, dreams, and prayers.[28] For Luke the Holy Spirit is continuously active in and through God's kingdom outpost in response to prayer. As Luke tells it, the Jesus story begins with a "pentad of prayers."[29] Perhaps the simplest, yet most profound prayer is Mary's cry of humble submission (Luke 1:38). It shows that prayer is response. As Peterson notes, "Someone has spoken to us, before we open our mouths, whether we remember or are aware of it or not."[30]

Luke continues his story by narrating numerous stories about prayer. Three of these are unique to Luke: the neighbor at prayer (Luke 11:5-13), the widow (Luke 18:1-8), and the "sinner" (Luke 18:9-14). Luke emphasizes prayer as the power to persevere as God's people in an alien world. There are no formal rituals, persons or places that have priority. The neighbor teaches us that we pray whenever we have an inclination for it. Prayer, like our relationship with God, is unpredictable, unplanned and unrehearsed.[31]

The messiah told parables about persevering in prayer because that is what he did as he lived as God's anointed in a rebellious age. Jesus received the Holy Spirit in prayer (Luke 3:22). Led by the Spirit, Jesus prayed and fasted for forty days in the wilderness (Luke 4:1-2). Jesus prayed while performing miracles (Luke 9:16; John 11:41-42). It was while at prayer that Jesus was transfigured (Luke 9:28-29). Because

Jesus habitually withdrew for a season of prayer (Luke 5:16), it is hardly surprising that when this evil age claimed its greatest victory Jesus died with a prayer on his lips (Luke 23:46).

Just as the Gospel of Luke opens with prayer, so does Acts (Luke 1:10; 24:53; Acts 1:14). The story of the Spirit and prayer continues in God's alien community. As it struggles in the shadows of the second coming, the divine gifts of Spirit and prayer sustain and guide it. The early church, because it still shared in the fallenness of this age, struggled with racism, lack of vision, and faltering courage. Yet in Luke's narrative God unleashed his empowering Spirit in response to even the faintest cry for the kingdom.

These disciples "devoted themselves…to prayers" (Acts 2:42). After Peter and John were dragged before the high court, this band of renegades "raised their voices together in prayer" (Acts 4:24) and God filled them with the Spirit to speak "boldly" (4:31). The twelve lead the beginning community from their knees (Acts 6:4). Stephen followed his Lord's example by dying with a prayer on his lips (Acts 7:59). God raised Dorcas from the dead in response to Peter's cry (Acts 9:40). God confronted the church's latent racism that kept her from embracing Gentiles while Peter was at his noon prayer (Acts 10:9). In fact Luke fashions the entire Cornelius episode as response to prayer (Acts 10:2, 9, 30-31).[32] Congregational leadership was hammered out only through "prayer and fasting" (Acts 14:23).

Prayer saturates the ministry of Paul in Acts. He seeks a place of prayer in Philippi (Acts 16:13, 16). While in prison he and Silas pray and sing (Acts 16:25). At his parting from the Ephesian elders "he knelt down with them all and prayed" (Acts 16:36). After spending a week with believers in Tyre he "knelt to pray" (Acts 21:5) before departing. In Jerusalem, while at prayer in the temple, Jesus spoke to Paul (Acts 22:17). In the middle of a storm at sea Paul mysteriously breaks bread and prays (Acts 27:35-36). While stranded on Malta Paul learns that Publius' father was sick, and after crying for the kingdom, he healed him (Acts 28:8).

The language of prayer pervades Luke's tale of the faithful community. The language is neither forced nor contrived. Rather, like a friend going to another friend, prayer is the "natural, unselfconscious language" of the body longing for the consummation of the kingdom.[33]

Though perhaps unrecognized, Paul's epistles are laden with prayer for the community of Christ. Every epistle that bears his name has at least one prayer, including little Philemon (Phm 25).[34] Continuing an Old Testament tradition, Paul places heavy emphasis on petitionary prayer. "Do not be anxious about anything," Paul exhorts the Philippians, "but in everything, by prayer and petition, with thanksgiving, present your requests to God" (Phil 4:4-6).

Petition takes on an eschatological twist in Paul's writings as well. The first fruits of the new age, the resurrection of Jesus and the presence of the Holy Spirit, have already been graciously granted by the Father. These events fuel the cries of faith for God to complete his task in the world. This goal lies behind the yearning of the sojourning community to know Christ "and the power of his resurrection" (Phil 3:10). Life, even prayer, is recast in light of God's heavenward goal (Phil 3:14).

Many strands of biblical theology on prayer are woven into a remarkable story told three times in the Old Testament: Hezekiah's illness, prayer and healing (2 Kgs 20:1-11; 2 Chr 32:24-26; Isa 38:1-8). The story is breathtaking in the claims it makes for prayer. Isaiah delivers an unambiguous message to Hezekiah. He is to put his house in order "because you are going to die; you will not recover" (2 Kgs 20:1). Rather than resigning to his fate, Hezekiah promptly went to the Lord in fervent prayer. "Remember, O LORD, how I have walked before you," he lamented. He wept "bitterly" in his petitions to the God of Israel. Before the prophet even got out of the courtyard, God told Isaiah, "Go back and tell Hezekiah….'This is what the LORD, the God of your father David says: I have heard your prayer and seen your tears; I will heal you'" (2 Kgs 20.5).

Prayer literally altered the future, not only for Hezekiah but also for God's people. God used Hezekiah's prayer as wool to weave a different future, which he allowed his child to co-author. The cry of his children has a profound impact upon the God who reveals himself as a loving Father. The Father shows the respect he has for his creatures by including them, through prayer, in accomplishing the divine agenda for the world.[35] What a profound gift of grace to humanity!

CULTIVATING A SACRED GARDEN FOR PRAYER

We are not experts in prayer. Our inner being is often chaotic. Our sinful nature overshadows our virtue. Our world is unjust and to our horror we often share in that injustice. So we pray. We pray because we are powerless. We cry because we mourn our fallenness. We flee to the garden of prayer because there we learn of the way God wills the world to be. In that sacred place we discover the tender embrace of our Father.

Crying for Embrace

Harding understood that prayer is fundamentally about relationship. This is not a yearning we create. Rather it is the work of God's own Spirit in and through us. God's steadfast love stalks us like a lion on the hunt (Ps 23:6). Such love is relentless until we are caught up within it. Embracing our Father in prayer begins with the truth few disciples even dare to imagine: our Father loves us as much as he loves Jesus![36] He gave Jesus up on the cross in order to have fellowship with us.

We cry for divine embrace when we surrender ourselves to the Spirit who has been poured out into our hearts. He leads us into intimacy by inspiring us to cry "Abba, Father." Through our prayer embrace we learn the meaning of God's invitation to follow him into the desert where he will "speak tenderly" (Hos 2:14) to us. There we will learn to call him our "husband," not merely "master" (Hos 2:16).

Building time into our schedule for a getaway with God is crucial. The saints throughout Scripture, and Jesus himself, maintained a rhythm of prayer. Relationships are cultivated deliberately. So setting specific times in which we can be alone with the lover of our souls is essential to the maintenance of our romance. We soon discover that through a regular rhythm of simply embracing God in prayer our inner chaos gives way to order as we adore the Father and he delights in us.

Crying for Redemption

Prayer is more than seeking the embrace of the Lord; it is also the cry of God's people for redemption. With creation groaning under the curse of sin and our purest motives tainted with evil, we lament. In prayer we thus ask the Lord of mercies, because of the power of the cross, to make the world right, to make us right, to restore *shalom* to this haunted world. We join with the saints of old in prayer

> Lord! You are mindful of our guilt;
>   you know our ways.
> Do not remember our sins,
>   for your name's sake, Lord!
> Spare, Lord, spare your people; with your
>   precious blood you have redeemed the world.
> Do not be angry with us forever.
> Lord, have mercy on us![37]

Crying for redemption, lamenting our sin, is a great act of faith and hope. It is rooted in the supreme faith that the God who delivers loves and cares for his own and will intervene and alter the future by changing the present.

Crying for Wisdom and Power

To pray is to walk in the light of God's gentle embrace, confessing, without holding back, "God I don't know what to do and if I did I don't know if I could do it." As we struggle to be "resident aliens," we find we do not have the internal resources to be in the world but not of the world. We find it easier to make peace with the world. In our prayers, then, we cry for direction. We claim the prayer of Paul as our own, that God grant us "the Spirit of wisdom and revelation" that we may discern his will for our lives, our communities and his world (Eph 1:17-21; Jam 1:5).

But as God's people we need more than wisdom. We need power

to live and do God's will on earth as it is in heaven. Thus we again cry for supernatural power to course through our being and our kingdom outposts. We pray that God grant us the faith to claim the power that raised Jesus' dead body to life (Eph 1:20) to be focused in our inner being through the power of the Holy Spirit (Eph 3:16-21).

Crying with the Saints

Christian prayer is normally a personal exercise, but it is not a lonely discipline. Our prayer life finds strength, depth and power by remaining connected to the community of faith. Companionship in prayer is found in the Spirit who prays in and through us. But we also have another resource that is often overlooked. Christians pray with the saints. God's family includes all those "in heaven and on earth" (Eph 3:14) who compose "a great cloud of witnesses" (Heb 12:1) who have struggled on their knees. These prayer warriors have providentially left gifts of gold for the family of God.

We claim their faith first by praying Scripture itself. Harding believed prayer was especially powerful when combined with Scripture. Millions of believers down through history have discovered the same power. Moses found boldness before God when he simply brought God's word back to him (Num 14:17-19).[38] Scripture becomes a powerful means of grace though which God himself opens our mouths to pray. Scripture can give us the very words we need to pray in times of great spiritual drought or pain. Cultivating times of praying the Psalms, the Lord's Prayer, and many other texts can greatly enrich our experience of prayer.

We also can claim the wisdom of the ages through collections of prayers. God's people have always been like Israel, people who "wrestle with God" (Gen 32:28; Col 4:12). Many prayers have been preserved, not because they are works of art, but because the words were helpful in wrestling with God in prayer. In the Psalter, the Songs of Ascent (Pss 120-134) were a mini-prayer book for a pilgrimage. Some prayer books follow specific rhythms that help provide a cadence for our journey. We have discovered that they can be especially helpful for planning a "getaway" with God, a spiritual retreat.

CONCLUSION

The NBST believed prayer was essential to living in the kingdom of God. Prayer is not a mere command or symbolic form that disciples perform. Rather, prayer is the life blood of the church. Through prayer the sojourning community finds that God mysteriously unleashes divine power in response. Through prayer the Lord of history invites his children to help write history. What a great honor he has granted us.

Observe how God creates the future with you by keeping a prayer journal. Harding appealed to his life experiences frequently as proof that God hears our prayers and moves in miraculous ways. By journaling we weave the fabric of the Spirit into our own histories with God. We can go back and see the hand of God working in and though our prayers. The journal becomes both a witness to prayer and feeds future prayer. Truly prayer is a means of grace.

DISCUSSION QUESTIONS

1. If you had been in a discussion with L. S. White how would you have responded to being "warped" by Mueller's trust theory? What Harding/Mueller prayer moments have you had in your life?

2. How does our view of God effect our prayer life?

3. How is prayer crying for the kingdom? How does that influence what we pray for?

4. How can praying the Scriptures enrich our embrace with God? Choose Psalm 23 or Psalm 42-43 or the Lord's Prayer to pray for a week, how has it blessed you?

CHALLENGES

Plan a spiritual getaway where you pray through the Psalms or a book like *The Prymer.*

Decide this week that you will awake ten minutes early for a period of prayer in which you do nothing but adore God.

Begin a prayer journal this week.

PRAYER

Abba, Father. You are truly beautiful and lovely. We long for your embrace in our lives and our communities. Yet we confess that prayer is difficult for us. We ask that you grant us eyes to discern your holy presence with us. Fill us with your Holy Spirit to give us strength for the day and insight to make decisions consistent with your will. Most of all Father we cling to the promise of redemption that you have already granted us through the death, and resurrection, of our brother. Come quickly, Lord Jesus. Amen.

RESOURCES

C. Leonard Allen, *The Contemporaries Meet the Classics on Prayer* (West Monroe, LA: Howard, 2003)

Richard J. Foster, *Prayer: Finding the Heart's True Home* (San Francisco: HarperSanFrancisco, 1992)

J. H. Garrison, *Alone with God, A Manuel of Devotions,* ed. Gary Holloway (Siloam Springs, AR: Leafwood, 2003)

Stanley J. Grenz, *Prayer: The Cry for the Kingdom*, rev. ed (Grand Rapids: Eerdmans, 2005)

The Prymer, translated and adapted by Robert E. Webber (Brewster, MA: Paraclete, 2000)

Gary Holloway and Earl Lavender, *Living God's Love: An Invitation to Christian Spirituality* (Siloam Springs, AR: Leafwood, 2004)

PART III

KINGDOM LIFE: FREE TO SERVE

The "apocalyptic" theology of the NBST stresses the continuing acts of God in the world for the sake of his kingdom. God takes special care of his kingdom people who reside as aliens in the world by providing all their needs. He dwells in us through the Spirit as an enabling power for the purpose of transforming us into his own likeness. The Spirit uses specific means of grace to accomplish this transformation. As we read the Bible daily, give alms to the poor, assemble around the table as a community on the Lord's day, and continue in daily prayer, the Father conforms us to the image of his Son.

This divine dynamic, rather than employing a human mechanism or following a prescribed plan or law, sets us free. It frees us to be kingdom people in this present evil age. The Spirit of God works to liberate us from the bondage of the fallen world. The NBST, as Boll illustrates below, saw this freedom as a central aspect of kingdom living.

> In some respects the bondage of law appeals to the flesh more than the freedom of the gospel. "It is far easier," says Adolph Harnack, "to live under any authority, even the hardest, than in the freedom of the good." Freedom is strenuous. It calls for thought, for principle, for heart-searchings, for decisions. Freedom stands in self-control as opposed to out-

> side control. The slave's life is easy in some respects. He is told what to do; and when he has done that, he is through. His master sees to all the problems of life for him. All he has to do is to follow orders. There are not a few Christians who would thank you to tell them exactly how much Bible reading they are expected to do every day, how many times a day they are to pray, exactly how much of their money they are to give, how much of Christian work they are to do, and exactly what work; also what they must not do—in short to have a rule and code of precepts which they are to perform, by which to keep out of hell and go to heaven. But the free Christian must ever seek the mind of his Lord: he must judge what is well-pleasing to Him, must study and think what love would do; and he cannot be content with the mere right and wrong: he must exceed those bounds; in short, he must follow Jesus.[1]

While this freedom is applicable to the whole range of transformed human existence in Christ, in this section we have chosen to concentrate on three important themes. First, the Christian is free from all national boundaries and allegiances to human institutions. This frees us to serve all humanity without the burden of divisive nationalistic commitments. Second, the Christian is free from creedal commitments constructed by human institutions. This frees us to discuss openly the meaning of kingdom without fear of institutional reprisals. We are free to think for ourselves, to think within community, and to pursue the kingdom of God without debilitating debt to mere human traditions. Third, the Christian is free from the Platonic dualism that demeans the goodness of creation. This frees us to serve the creation as we were originally intended and to live out our role in the world as divine imagers. Free from the law of sin and death that bound us to this fallen world, we pursue a life of love and freedom in the hope of the new creation.

NINE

THE PRINCE OF PEACE: PLEDGING ALLEGIANCE TO THE KINGDOM

Blessed are the peacemakers, for they will be called children of God.
—Jesus, Mt. 5:9

Ought our motto to be 'Our country, right or wrong?
—Alexander Campbell (1848)[1]

The chief occupation of human governments from the beginning has been war. Nine-tenths of the taxes paid by the human family, have gone to preparing for, carrying on, or paying the expenses of war.
—David Lipscomb (1889)[2]

Other than the fact that a war had been raging for sometime, it seemed like just another Lord's Day in Columbia, Tennessee. Yet on this Sunday an unusual guest appeared in the congregation wearing the insignia of the Confederate States of America. The officer was on a special mission from General Nathan Bedford Forrest to determine if David Lipscomb was guilty of treason against the Confederacy.

It was not the first time that Lipscomb had raised eyebrows. On one occasion as he was preaching a man called for twelve men to help him "string up the preacher." Lipscomb had declared that it was wrong for Christians to kill, even Yankees. A committee representing Churches of Christ in middle Tennessee had already petitioned the Confederate government for an exemption from conscription laws because Christians cannot participate in "bloody conflicts" which civil governments so frequently engage.[3]

When central Tennessee fell under Federal military authority a meeting was organized with Union officials. In this meeting David Lipscomb, among others, presented a similar request to the U.S. Army. The petitioners stated that "we recognize it as a solemn duty we owe to God to the government…save when that government requires of us something contrary to the letter and spirit of the Christian religion."[4]

So when General Forrest's officer arrived on Sunday morning Lipscomb was already suspect. But undeterred by the military presence, Lipscomb preached his lesson as faithfully as he knew how. When the officer reported on whether or not the sermon was treasonous, he said, "I have not reached a conclusion as to whether or not the doctrine of the sermon is loyal to the Southern Confederacy, but I am profoundly convinced that he is loyal to the Christian religion."[5]

A Peaceful Tradition

Though surprising to many, Churches of Christ have historically been a leading pacifist group in America.[6] Many of its pioneer leaders like Barton Stone, Alexander Campbell, Tolbert Fanning, and Moses Lard opposed warfare on Christian grounds. The NBST enriched and diversified this peace tradition.

The pacifism of the NBST was rooted in the vision of the kingdom outlined in chapter two.[7] God's kingdom sat in judgment upon the pretensions and ambitions of all human governments. Even the very best of human governments, even that of the United States, was at its root idolatrous and corrupt. The problem is not particular individuals but, as Lipscomb said, "the whole body politic."[8]

The "spirit" of God's kingdom and this age are completely incompatible. The spirit of civil government is "force, violence and destruction of life."[9] Lipscomb believed that war was "the rich man's war but the poor man's fight." The average citizen was "taxed and devoured by the sword to gratify the ambition of politicians, demagogues, and ambitious adventurers...who make their gains on the misfortune of their fellow man."[10] However, kingdom principles are "epitomized" in the Sermon on the Mount, where one learns to love and pray for enemies.[11] The relation of the resident alien to all human governments was simply to pay ones taxes and pray for peaceful lives.

Perhaps nothing illustrates the tenacity of the NBS peace tradition like the fate of J. N. Armstrong and Cordell Christian College. Armstrong had entered NBS in October 1893 and proved to be such a gifted Greek student that he took over Harding's class. Upon graduation in 1896 he remained as an instructor and followed Harding to begin Potter Bible College in 1901.[12] Along the way he married Harding's daughter, Woodson.

Armstrong arrived at Cordell as its second president in 1908. Under his able leadership Cordell grew into the largest college among Churches of Christ until it was killed by partisan citizens in 1918. The Cordell tragedy illustrated the truth which Lipscomb discerned years earlier that "civil power" would seek to "throttle the church, as it sought to destroy its founder," if it dared to oppose the state's agenda.[13]

Long before America officially entered World War I the government had been priming the pump. Government propaganda described the impending conflict as a struggle of light against darkness, virtue against sin, civilization against chaos, and God against the Devil. By the time the United States entered the war there was "xenophobic hatred of anything German."[14]

Congress granted sweeping powers to the federal government with the passage of the Espionage Act of June 15, 1917, which was soon followed by the Sedition Act of 1918. These laws empowered the government to fine a person $10,000 or imprison him for up to twenty years for disloyalty, discouraging enlistment or even unpatriotic criticism of the U.S. government.[15] Suddenly many members of the Churches of Christ were in danger of treasonous speech and behavior.

On April 6, 1917 the United States declared war on the Central Powers of Europe. Though Armstrong and most of the faculty took a conscientious objector stance, they attempted to be supportive of the government's cause through the purchase of liberty bonds.[16] But when some Cordell students were drafted and took noncombatant status the local draft board and defense council decided to investigate. Two students, Ben Randolph and Levi Kindrick Wilmeth, were sent to Ft. Leavenworth. They were "brow-beaten, warned they would be shot, blind folded, placed before a firing squad" if they did not give up their foolishness.[17] Another Cordell alumnus, a Mr. Smith, was arrested in Clovis, New Mexico on the charge of making unpatriotic comments about the flag.

The patriotic citizens of Cordell accused the college, and Armstrong in particular, of pro-German sentiments. Perhaps the greatest troubles began when S. A. Bell, a professor at Cordell Christian, published an article in the May 16, 1918 edition of Armstrong's paper *The Gospel Herald*. The journal was intercepted by the postmaster and forwarded to Washington D.C. on suspicion of violating the Espionage and Sedition Acts.

Special Agent J. G. Findley of the Bureau of Investigation (later the FBI) and the Washita County Council of Defense began a serious investigation of Cordell Christian College. Armstrong was summoned to appear before the council on July 12. He informed the board that though he had held to a pacifist position for twenty-six years he did believe it was permissible for the U.S. to fight a defensive war. Christians, however, were to take a noncombatant role even in a defensive war. On July 23 the council,

> issued an order to Cordell Christian that the board of regents and faculty be so re-organized as will unreservedly conform to all military policies and requirements of the government in the present war. All 'doctrines or teaching' in the school must 'comply strictly and to the fullest extent with the military policy of the government.'[18]

Armstrong offered his resignation to the board but it was rejected. But the end was near. Intense public pressure and threats of violence against the school brought the board to a difficult decision. Rather than be forced into a position it could not follow, the college, its faculty, and president became "martyrs" for conviction.[19] Thus for the crime of preaching "disloyal sermons" Armstrong and his college were destroyed.

In stark contrast to the peaceful tradition embraced by the NBS was the militarism of G. H. P. Showalter and the *Firm Foundation*. Conscientious objectors, according to Showalter, were German agents seeking to undermine the war effort. The church "should support the government" rather than these imposters.[20] Austin McGary directly attacked the pacifist theme of the NBS: "Nashville, Tennessee is the headquarters of that character of slackery. These sanctimonious fanatics claim that their 'citizenship is in heaven' in such an exclusive sense as will not admit of their being citizens of any nation."[21]

Even the *Gospel Advocate*, no longer under Lipscomb's guidance, became unfriendly to the peace position. Lee Douglas, district attorney for Middle Tennessee, threatened to arrest *Advocate* publisher J. C. McQuiddy for the seditious effect his journal had upon young men. McQuiddy closed the *Advocate* to articles promoting noncombatant positions. At the same time he urged disciples to "be careful that they do not say anything against the government of the United States."[22]

R. L. Whiteside, a former NBS student, symbolizes the transition made by Churches of Christ away from the apocalyptic peace tradition. Quietly rejecting Lipscomb's pacifism by 1895, he became a more vocal opponent as the years progressed.[23] With the threat of prison removed many antiwar preachers began to speak up following the First World War. Whiteside admonished them to "keep as quiet as you were during the war."[24] Pacifists were stereotyped as anarchists who undermined national security and would stand "idly by while a fiend raped and murdered his wife."[25] By 1934 Whiteside had embraced utter contempt for the historic position embraced by the NBS. He wrote bitterly: "[T]his treatise is to show that the doctrine of pacifism is a hiding place of false doctrine, and to answer with logic and scripture the claims and the creed of this nondescript religio-politico cult, showing the views to be unethical and unbiblical and in all respects untrue."[26]

Lipscomb had said that the spirit of Christianity and the spirit of war were antithetical. These two spirits are seen in the remnants of the pacifist position in Leo Boles and the emerging consensus in Whiteside. Boles declared, in line with the NBST, that the "altruistic spirit is the spirit of Christianity....Vicarious suffering must be endured in order to live the Christian life."[27] Whiteside, and the majority of people in Churches of Christ, had by now rejected such a spirit. Whiteside, reflecting the humanistic impulse of his perspective, rejected pacifism because, he wrote, "the law of self-preservation is embedded in our nature."[28]

Foy E. Wallace, Jr., who embraced Whiteside's views on war, suggested that H. Leo Boles and R. L. Whiteside should debate the issue.[29] The debate never happened. By that time there was no need for it. The heritage of apocalyptic peace had virtually vanished in a church that was increasingly at home in its American culture.

GOD'S VISION OF PEACE

Though filled with battle scenes, Scripture, even through a casual reading, reveals that God did not create war. War is symptomatic of the fall of humanity and the destruction of God's *shalom*. The messiah's brother wrote: "Where do these wars and battles between yourselves first start? You want something and you haven't got it; so you are prepared to kill. You have an ambition that you cannot satisfy; so you fight to get your way by force" (James 4:1-2, Jerusalem Bible). War is the expression of Satanic currents in this age—greed, unchecked ambition, absence of love for our neighbor. War is an enemy of God that will be abolished when the kingdom fully arrives out of its present shadows.

Scripture also makes it clear that God has used war to accomplish his divine purpose as evil punishes evil. The Old Testament in particular reveals that the Lord of history has, in his providence, used a dirty tool to accomplish a dirty task. For example, Lipscomb believed that God had used the Civil War as his "battle axe" to destroy the evil of slavery.[30] But contrary to many popular opinions the Old Testament is no carte blanc justification for Christian participation in carnal warfare.[31]

The paradigmatic moment for Israel was the Exodus. The Exodus functions in the Old Testament in a manner similar to Golgotha in the New. Here Yahweh redeemed and claimed Israel as his own. A great battle took place. What may be missed however is that it was not a battle between Israelite and Egyptian, but a battle between Yahweh and "the gods of Egypt" (Ex 12:12; cf. 15:11; 18:11). "But Moses said to the people, 'Do not be afraid, stand firm, and see the deliverance that the LORD will accomplish for you today; for the Egyptians whom you see today you shall never see again. The LORD will fight for you, you have only to keep still'" (Ex 14:13-14). The account of the Exodus is clear on one important point—the Israelites did nothing to bring about the destruction of the Egyptians. Though they will "see" God bring salvation they do not lay a hand on an Egyptian. Thus, at its foundational moment Israel is excluded from contributing to her salvation by fighting for it. The Exodus was not a "natural" war but a supernatural intervention by Yahweh to defeat the enemies of his people.

Much the same could be said about the narratives of war in Joshua.[32] Though Israel did participate in the battles in the conquest, these do not seem to have served a normative function. These battles never served as an absolute ethic for war. Israel functioned, in these battles, in God's providence as the Lord's instrument of judgment upon the sin of the Canaanites (cf. Gen 15:16).

The way battles were fought in the Old Testament is illustrated in 2 Chronicles 20. If Israel trusted in Yahweh then battles would be like the Exodus. As the Lord of Hosts says:

> You will not have to fight this battle. Take up your positions; stand firm and see the deliverance the LORD will give you, O Judah and Jerusalem. Do not be afraid; do not be discouraged. Go out to face them tomorrow, and the LORD will be with you. (2 Chr 20:17)

So the next day the people head out following the Levitical priests and musicians to the "front." When Judah arrived on the scene they found the enemy had slain each other (20:22-26). As in the Exodus, when Israel trusted in the Lord, they never laid a hand on anyone (cf. Jdgs 7).

The prophets of Israel sensed a greater future for God's creation. Rather than simply use war to bring about his purpose (Jer 50-51) or regulate it as he did in the Torah (Deut 20), God would abolish it completely.

> He will judge between many peoples
> and will settle disputes for strong nations far and wide.
> They will beat their swords into plowshares
> and their spears into pruning hooks.
> Nation will not take up sword against nation,
> nor will they train for war anymore.
> (Micah 4:3; cf. Isa 2:4)

The post-exilic prophet Zechariah envisioned a future that included a peace-making king. The king would bring about the restoration of *shalom* that Micah had foreseen.

> See, your king comes to you,
> righteousness and having salvation
> gentle and riding on a donkey,
> on a colt, the foal of a donkey.
> I will take away the chariots from
> Ephraim and the war-horses from Jerusalem,
> and the battle bow will be broken.
> He will proclaim peace to the nations. (Zech 9:9-10)

Thus, while containing accounts of many battles, the Old Testament casts a vision of *shalom* or peace.[33] The instruments of war must be transformed into the implements of peace. This transformation, moreover, is accomplished by the very ones who possess weapons. As the prophet said, "*They* shall beat *their* swords into plowshares…" (Micah 4:3).

For the Christian, the Old Testament's vision for peace is taken up by Jesus of Nazareth. Zechariah had prophesied that a king unlike any other was on his way. He would not arrive in a caravan of limousines but in a beat up Yugo. He was a new kind of sovereign. He reigned by service and conquered by dying.

According to the New Testament Jesus battled the principalities and powers. His battle was not merely with Pharisees or Roman governors but against spiritual realities. Just as Yahweh met and defeated the gods of Egypt through a series of skirmishes culminating in his massive victory at the Red Sea, so too Jesus battled spiritual realities through his ministry, culminating in his decisive victory at the cross.

> None of the rulers of this age understood this [God's wisdom], for if they had, they would not have crucified the Lord of glory (1 Cor 2:8).

> He disarmed the rulers and authorities, and made a public spectacle of them, triumphing over them in it [the cross] (Col 2:15).

These powers, authorities and rulers are not primarily city council members. They are spiritual realities that manifest themselves in a variety of ways that may include civil government (Col 1:16-17; Eph 6:12).

Jesus's death authenticates and models his teaching. Our salvation—flowing from Calvary—was obtained, like Israel, without any contribution on our part. God fought the supernatural battle on our behalf. Disciples are called to follow the conquering methodology of their king: they love, pray for, serve and forgive their enemies.

Jesus's death embodies the teaching of his Sermon on the Mount. Jesus died a peacemaker and was called "the son of God" (Matt 5:9; 27:54). When he was struck in the face he did not strike back (5:39; 26:67). He loved his enemies and prayed for those who persecuted him (Matt 5:43; Luke 23:34). Thus death of Jesus exemplifies the qualities that are normative for disciples in the kingdom of God.[34]

The pattern of suffering love continues into the epistles. The death of Jesus is interpreted as a peace initiative on the part of God.

> God demonstrates his own love for us in this: While we were still sinners Christ died for us. Since we have now been justified by his blood, how much more shall we be saved from God's wrath through him! For if, when we were God's enemies, we were reconciled to him through the death of his Son, how much more, having been reconciled, shall we be saved through his life (Rom 5:8-10, NIV)

Profound ethical implications flow from Paul's claims to those who would call God "Father." Those reconciled and adopted into the family have their lives reshaped in Christ to deal with enemies in the same manner that our elder brother did. This is clearly demonstrated by Paul later in the same epistle. In a passage that echoes Jesus' teaching in the Sermon on the Mount, Paul orders life in the kingdom with principles drawn from that sermon.

> Bless those who persecute you; bless and do not curse....Live in harmony with one another....Do not repay anyone evil for evil. Be careful to do what is right in the eyes of everybody. If it is possible, as far as it depends on you, live at peace with everyone. Do not take revenge, my friends, but leave room for God's wrath, for it is written: 'It is mine to avenge; I will repay,' says the Lord. On the contrary: 'If your enemy is hungry, feed him; if he is thirsty, give him something to drink. In doing this, you will heap burning coals on his head.' Do not be overcome by evil, but overcome evil with good (Rom 12:14, 15, 17-21, NIV).

After surveying the Pauline corpus, Richard Hays concludes that "there is not a syllable in the Pauline letters that can be cited in support of Christians employing violence."[35]

The Hebrews's writer also bears witness to a community shaped profoundly by the pattern of Jesus' teaching and death. The writer recalls the earlier painful experiences the disciples had endured for the sake of their faith:

> But recall those earlier days when, after you had been enlightened, you endured a hard struggle with sufferings, sometimes being publicly exposed to abuse and persecution, and sometimes being partners with those so treated. For you had compassion for those who were in prison, and you cheerfully accepted the plundering of your possessions, knowing that you yourselves possessed something better and more lasting. (Heb 10:32-34)

These disciples endured persecution with an eye on the coming kingdom. They faithfully embraced God's vision of *shalom* in the present because of their hope in the future.

Peter speaks to God's band of renegades along the Black Sea in words that frighten many modern disciples. His is certainly a different cast to discipleship than what is seen in many contemporary forms of Christianity. He calls disciples to peaceful, hopeful, endurance as aliens in a hostile environment. Peter's hope is, once again, grounded in Golgotha and the *eschaton.*

> Beloved, do not be surprised at the fiery ordeal that is taking place among you to test you, as though something strange were happening to you. But rejoice insofar as you are sharing Christ's sufferings, so that you may also be glad and shout for joy when his glory is revealed. If you are reviled for the name of Christ, you are blessed, because the spirit of glory which is the Spirit of God, is resting on you....Yet if any of you suffers as a Christian, do not consider it a disgrace, but glory God because you bear his name (1 Pet 4:12-16; cf. 1:6-7; 3:13-18; 5. 8-10).

The witness of the New Testament is consistently against violence. Indeed, God's kingdom outpost, like the one who established it, is called to endure and accept suffering rather than inflict it as it follows the example of its reigning king. We follow Jesus to the cross (Mk 8:34). The church is a sign of God's *shalom*, a display case arranged by God showing what the world will look like when his kingdom is manifest in its glory.[36]

BECOMING PEOPLE OF PEACE

The early church was not able to live as a kingdom of peace through sheer will power. It was, rather, through constant communion with the Prince of Peace that crucifixion of the sinful nature took place. Peace is ultimately a grace of the Holy Spirit (Gal. 5:22). Through the ministry of the Spirit we come to realize that we belong to a family that transcends any national, racial, or gender boundaries. We offer the following starting points as suggestions for embracing God's vision of peace for his world.

Seek first the Kingdom

"Seek first his kingdom and his righteousness" (Mt. 6:33) is the clarion call for the body of Christ. A positive step toward embodying Christ in the world is to recover the Sermon on the Mount as a serious basis for Christian ethics. Many believers through the centuries have blunted the force of this sermon. Some claim it was merely an "interim" ethic, others that it was limited to the apostles on a special mission, and some have stated that it was simply part of the "old covenant" and therefore "abolished." Others, like Reinhold Niebuhr, simply concluded that Jesus teaching was not relevant to modern life.

Our survey of the New Testament reveals that Paul, Peter and the Hebrews' writer believed and taught the precepts of the Sermon to their converts. As Lipscomb pointed out years ago, "who can study the New Testament…the admonitions of the Holy Spirit speaking through the apostles and for a moment doubt, that Christ specifically gave this sermon to regulate the hearts and lives of his followers." Indeed, when we abandon the Sermon as the basis for discipleship, "the spirit of Christ is driven out of the church" and a "spirit of the world" creeps in.[37]

Recovering the Sermon as the agenda-setter for the community of God reorients us and brings balance to our journey. The sermon forces us to deal with life issues, public and private, in light of God's in-breaking kingdom. Instead of narrowly defining our identity in terms of ecclesiastical forms, we center our identity in kingdom righteousness. As kingdom people we follow Jesus and are identified by our discipleship.

The sermon is radical and we do utterly fail to live it. But that is why the NBST urges us to cling for our lives to the grace of God while we cry for the Spirit to empower us to live beyond our fallen capabilities.

Seeking first the kingdom also means avoiding giving religious justification for war. Lipscomb said, "When religious people engage in war, they clothe their strife with the frenzy of religious fanaticism. Then it makes war more bitter, more bloody, more cruel, more vindictive in its character."[38] The history of war from the Crusades to terrorist Jihad bears witness to the truth of Lipscomb's comments. Seeking God's kingdom, however, is to seek nothing less than the establishment of *shalom*.

Prophetic Eyes

So ingrained is nationalism in some communities of faith that some, it seems, lift up patriotism as a fruit of the Spirit.[39] Lee Camp proposes a mental exercise that is helpful in recovering the prophetic eyes necessary for peaceful living. Do we American Christians see ourselves as *American* Christians, or as American *Christians*?[40] Where does our fundamental identity lie? Is it in the word American, or in the word Christian?

If our identity is rooted first in the word Christian, we then have the resources to step back and evaluate the state through the prophetic eyes of the kingdom. Few people have been as grateful as Alexander Campbell for his American heritage. Yet when the United States invaded Mexico, unjustly in Campbell's opinion, he was forced to ask, "ought our motto to be 'our country right or wrong?'"

Bartolome de Las Casas was a proud Spaniard. Las Casas arrived in what is now Haiti in 1502 as a missionary to the "wretched beings" that inhabited the island. Las Casas was confronted with the barbarism of colonial imperialism. In a protest written to the crown he said:

> It is my considered opinion that the greatest obstacle that stands in the way…is the harshness and cruelty of the treatment meted out by 'Christians' to those who surrender. This has been so harsh and so brutal that nothing is more odious nor more terrifying to the people than the name 'Christian', a word for which they use in their language the term *yares*, which means 'demons.'[41]

Las Casas prophetic critique of Spain was rooted in his love for his homeland. "My deep love of Castile has also been a spur, for I do not wish to see my country destroyed as a divine punishment for sins against the honour of God and the True Faith."[42]

Like Campbell, Lipscomb and Armstrong, Las Casas decided it was not "my country right or wrong" no matter what. Rather it was God and his kingdom. He evaluated his country's policies through the shadows of the coming kingdom. To evaluate our country through prophetic kingdom eyes is never an easy or popular task. To disagree with a course of action one's nation has taken is branded as unpatriotic or, as in the case of Armstrong, seditious.

The failure to subject the state to prophetic criticism has led to unimaginable injustice, even in the name of Christ. If other disciples had looked at the Spanish government's actions through kingdom eyes, Las Casas would never have had to protest. If American disciples would have evaluated culture through the coming kingdom, slavery and Jim Crow would have existed. If German disciples would have risen above nationalism, Hitler and the Holocaust might have been thwarted.

Prophetic eyes keep us from identifying the United States, or any other nation or ethnic group, with the kingdom of God. As Alexander Campbell said, "The American Nation as a nation is no more in spirit

Christian than were Greece and Rome."[43] Rather, God's kingdom stands in judgment upon all nations.

Peaceful Engagement

Disciples are called to be peacemakers. This, however, does not necessarily mean passive disengagement from the world around us. Our example is our Father who loved the world and gave his Son for it. This is radical engagement.[44] Recent examples of peaceful engagement are Ghandi and Martin Luther King, Jr. Nonviolent action had far reaching effect on the people of India. Ironically King, who modeled the principles of the peaceful kingdom in profound ways, was often called a communist and anarchist by Christians. The secret to his witness was the faith he confessed in his Nobel Peace Prize acceptance speech: "I believe that unarmed truth and unconditional love will have the final words in reality. That is why right temporarily defeated is stronger than evil triumphant."[45]

Rather than withdrawing from the world, disciples follow the Lamb's conquering methodology to love and serve the world. We can do this on many levels. One level could be working for legislation that cultivates peace. Rather than just protest nuclear, chemical and biological proliferation among "rogue" states, peacemakers protest the existence of these weapons themselves. Christians even promote alternatives to war such as international tribunals to settle disputes. Over one hundred and fifty years ago Alexander Campbell, in his dismay over U.S. aggression towards Mexico, called for the creation of "a congress of nations and a high court of nations for adjudicating and terminating all international misunderstandings and complaints, redressing and remedying all wrongs and grievances?"[46] This would demand the surrender of some national interests for the sake of peace, but Christ has already shown disciples this is how he works (Phil 2:6-11).

Disciples of peace, however, fundamentally seek *shalom* in the world through crying for the kingdom. We ask the Father to accomplish his will on earth just as he does in heaven. Prayer, as we have seen, is the Christian's "secret weapon." The prayers of peaceful disciples are more powerful than any bomb, space-based missile defense, or terrorist organization.

CONCLUSION

Perhaps R. L. Whiteside was correct. Self-preservation is naturally embedded in us. But Christians are called to live supernaturally rather than naturally (Rom 7-8). We realize that being a peaceable kingdom is a tall order. We likewise do not harbor utopian dreams that fallen humanity will embrace God's *shalom*. But that is not the issue. The issue is whether God's people will model for fallen humanity what God dreams for them. Will the world see an alternative to hate, "ethnic cleansing," and beheadings in the name of deity. We believe the church should be that alternative. In the church we love our enemies. In the church we pray for those who would do us evil. In the church when we are insulted we seek reconciliation. In the church we seek the kingdom and God's righteousness first.

We seek these things in our alien community not out of self-righteousness but precisely because we—as the haters, adulterers, murderers—have come face to face with the crucified God and heard him pray "Father forgive them." Our hates and self-serving agendas died with the Suffering Servant and we have been freed from them.

DISCUSSION QUESTIONS

1. What about the Cordell Christian College episode surprises you most? Do you believe Armstrong was disloyal to his country?

2. Does Scripture cast a "vision of peace" for disciples to embrace? In what ways can we embody peace in our churches, our communities, and our nation?

3. What can we learn about peaceful engagement from people like Las Casas, Ghandi, and Martin Luther King?

CHALLENGES

Read a challenging book like Richard Hughes' *Myths America Lives By*.

Pursue a sustained, in-depth, study of Jesus' Sermon on the Mount

Evaluate the world's military expenditures through prophetic eyes.

PRAYER

O Father, our hearts are torn. We desperately want to know and serve you in your kingdom. The pull of this age is powerful and narcotic and we cannot escape it. Give us the courage of Armstrong and Las Casas to stand for your kingdom. Give us the power through your Holy Spirit to walk the narrow path. We implore your grace for our failure to be a city on a hill that cannot be hid. Thank you for being our God and our Redeemer. Amen.

RESOURCES

Roland Bainton, *Christian Attitudes Toward War and Peace* (Nashville: Abingdon, 1979)

Lee Camp, *Mere Discipleship: Radical Christianity in a Rebellious World* (Grand Rapids: Brazos, 2003).

Edwin S. Gaustad, *Proclaim Liberty Throughout the Land: A History of Church and State in America* (New York: Oxford University Press, 1999, 2003)

Richard T. Hughes, *Myths America Lives By* (Urbana and Chicago: University of Illinois,2003)

John Howard Yoder, *When War is Unjust: Being Honest in Just-War Thinking*, rev. ed. (Maryknoll, NY: Orbis, 1996)

TEN

NO CREED BUT CHRIST: FREEDOM TO THINK AND SPEAK

It is for freedom that Christ has set you free. Stand firm, then, and do not let yourselves be burdened again by a yoke of slavery.
—Paul, *Galatians* 5:1

The fatal error of all reformers, has been that they have too hastily concluded that they knew the whole truth, and have settled back upon the same principles of proscription, intolerance and persecution, against which they so strongly remonstrated.
—John Rogers (1830)[1]

There is a great need to stress the importance of maintaining freedom of speech in the kingdom of God. Intolerance is dangerous to the future growth of the church....All progress of truth—scientific truth, political truth, or religious truth—all truth—has always depended on free speech and progressive teachers who were not afraid to teach their honest convictions.
—J. N. Armstrong[2]

In the early 1890s an intramural dispute arose between the front page editor of the *Gospel Advocate* and the *Baptist and Reflector*. F. D. Srygley was informed that Churches of Christ ought to agree with one another, that they should not have any differences. Srygley was part of a group that valued freedom to study, to explore and to express contrary points of view. The *Gospel Advocate* had long had a tradition of open discussion on all matters. David Lipscomb's openness was visible when he invited J. B. Higbee, a staunch supporter of the Missionary Society, to join the editorial staff in 1881. Srygley himself had clashed with Lipscomb on the same issues but was welcomed by Lipscomb as front page editor in 1889.[3] So open was Lipscomb's *Advocate* that he even let Selina Holman, whose articles gave him "the blues," argue for a wider role of women in the church.[4] Only truth suffered from censorship and creedalism in the tradition of Lipscomb.

Reflecting that radical commitment to freedom of thought, Srygley responded to his critics that because we differ in opinions and even argue is no indication we are not united. Further, he suggested that "we have never proposed or desired to unite Christians in any institution that is too narrow to allow them to differ in opinion or argue with each other." He continued saying, "we are in favor of giving everybody room to think and liberty to speak for himself." Christians can exercise such liberty, according to Srygley, because they are amenable only to the Lordship of Christ. Our union with one another, he insisted, is not dependent upon agreement on a myriad of opinions about scriptural issues. Rather, he stated passionately: "The basis of our union ought always be as broad as the conditions of salvation. No man has any right to make his plea for union narrower than this. It is wrong to make anything a condition of fellowship which is not essential to salvation. We draw the line here."[5]

ARMSTRONG AND BOLL: THE QUEST FOR FREEDOM

The Stone-Campbell Movement was born with a hunger for unity and a thirst for freedom.[6] Barton Stone had protested the power of denominational machinery over the consciences of the people. Rather than be bound by creeds people should have "free course to the Bible."[7] Thomas Campbell, who had experienced the high handedness of ecclesiastical bigotry, declared it was "high time for us not only to think, but to act, for ourselves." Through sad experience he had decided that "no man can be judged for his brother," therefore "every man must be allowed to judge for himself."[8]

The NBST embraced this heritage of freedom. Rather than seeing discipleship as a station, it believed disciples were on a grand faith odyssey. Thus when Lipscomb received a question from R. C. Horn of Texas about fellowshipping those with whom he disagreed, he replied that "we are never willing to give a man up finally, until he has committed the sin unto death." Lipscomb said he would honor such a person as family "so long as a man really desires to do right, to serve the Lord, to obey his commands we cannot withdraw from him. We are willing to accept him as a brother, no matter how ignorant, he may be, or how far short of the perfect standard his life may fall." Lipscomb rooted such a magnanimous attitude precisely in the recognition of his own sinfulness before the perfect and holy One. "Why should I not," he told Horn, "when I fall so short of the perfect knowledge myself? How do I know that the line beyond which ignorance damns, is behind me, not before me?"[9] If we show no mercy, then how do we expect God to show us mercy?

Tolerance and free discussion was standard fare at the NBS. For example, James A. Harding wanted his students to hear a perspective contrary to his and Lipscomb on civil government. He did not know who to get, so R. L. Whiteside suggested G. G. Taylor, who strongly disagreed with Harding and Lipscomb. As Whiteside recalled, Taylor lectured to the students, in front of both Lipscomb and Harding, "and no man ever received a more courteous hearing."[10]

Two students who drank deeply from this well of Christian freedom were J. N. Armstrong and R. H. Boll. Though these two could not have known it, their early training in freedom would cost them dearly as the twentieth century progressed.

The issue that tested the Churches of Christ's commitment to freedom was premillennialism. In the nineteenth century there was no standard position on eschatology for Churches of Christ. Barton Stone, Walter Scott, James Challen,[11] Moses Lard,[12] T. W. Brents,[13] and James A. Harding were all classical premillennialists. Alexander Campbell was a postmillennialist. There was considerable tolerance on eschatology, but one does not find any amillennialists in the nineteenth century.[14] Armstrong and Boll embraced a premillennial view.

The tolerance and freedom of the nineteenth century gave way to intolerance and power plays as Churches of Christ continued to shed the apocalyptic worldview. The skirmishes of Harding with Holloway (Holy Spirit) and White (prayer and providence) were harbingers of things to come. As a protégé of Harding, Boll had served as associate editor of *The Way*, *The Gospel Review* and *The Gospel Guide* and in 1909 became the front page editor for the *Gospel Advocate*. By 1914 Boll was one of the most popular writers and preachers in Churches of Christ. Trouble did not start for Boll until he began a five-part series on Revelation in which he contended for a literal approach to the book.[15]

Controversy soon erupted among fellow contributors to the *Advocate*. He was urged to stop writing on prophetic themes. Boll, who did write on other themes, refused to be coerced into a position that took away his freedom to speak as he believed. The prophetic literature was part of the canon and should be studied because it was God's word. In an unpublished article he stated that eschatology was important because it holds the "key to much of the motive-power of the Christian life."[16]

In rapid succession Boll's association with the *Advocate* was severed, renewed, and then severed permanently. Boll purchased *The Word and Work* in which he both defended himself and advanced his understanding of Scripture. But Boll was a marked man. The encroachments upon freedom decried by the pioneers surfaced with a vengeance. To remain in good standing M. C. Kurfees demanded of Boll, "Do you subscribe to the position of the Advocate?" Boll was incredulous. "I will do no such thing, I do not know what the 'position' of the Advocate is, or might turn out to be. I can subscribe to nothing and nobody except Jesus Christ."[17] Boll refused to surrender his freedom to think and speak.

Caught in the middle of this fight was J. N. Armstrong. He had long held the principle of freedom as it relates to Bible study. Freedom allowed one to explore and accept new truth as it was encountered. He exercised that freedom when he was persuaded to accept Harding's views on special providence.[18]

Armstrong had held for "thirty years, about the same position on the millennium that was held by Dr. T. W. Brents and James A. Harding."[19] Though agreeing on the millennium, Armstrong disagreed with Boll on various Scriptural interpretations. But the issue for Armstrong was not agreement but freedom. He believed that Boll had the right to think and speak. We did not, Armstrong argued, have to agree on this subject.

Late in 1924, E. M. Borden, an Oklahoma City preacher and editor of the *Herald of Truth*, led an assault upon Armstrong for his tolerance of Boll.[20] Armstrong, because he believed the course of the *Gospel Advocate* was wrong, had allowed Boll to publish in his journals *The Gospel Herald* and *The Living Message.* These journals had been modeled after the Lipscomb *Gospel Advocate* where full and free discussion could take place.[21] But the presence of Boll's articles "aroused a suspicion" in Borden.[22] Armstrong defended his course of action:

> I close this letter by reemphasizing the fact that my crime (?), is not that I hold to false doctrine respecting this matter...but my sin is that I have been unwilling to denounce, disfellowship, mark and avoid R. H. Boll for his position, and the teaching of that position on the kingdom....
>
> But I am not ready to withdraw my endorsement of, and cooperation with a man who is as tenacious in his determination to speak where the Bible speaks and to be silent where the Bible is silent, as I am, or as you are, and whose life measures up in every way in faithfulness to God as ours and whose disagreement with us is only the interpretation of some particular passage...which in no way affects faithfulness to God... No, Brother Borden, I cannot do that.[23]

Armstrong chides Borden. Surely he did not think Boll was the first to advocate a view on the millennium. Why persecute Boll when others had long held the same views? "Campbell, Brents and Harding have not been dead long enough for this," Armstrong exclaimed.[24]

"The thing that is now causing trouble," in Churches of Christ, Armstrong wrote, was not Boll's freedom of speech. Rather, it "is this divisive spirit, this self-righteous, dogmatic, intolerant spirit" that forces disciples to line up, shut up or suffer martyrdom.[25] He believed many simply failed to "recognize the enormity of the crime of causing division among the children of God."[26] Rather than suppress freedom the church should not let "trivial matters become a wedge for division."[27]

The crusade against Boll was just getting started, however. R. L. Whiteside teamed up with C. R. Nichol to produce a book that touched nerves throughout the church, *Christ and His Kingdom: A Review of R. H. Boll.*[28] Calling Boll's views "the slanderous ebullitions of a blasphemous blatherskite,"[29] Whiteside and Nichol zeroed in on Boll's view of the kingdom. The clashing worldviews emerge when they noted that Boll "draws a dark picture of the church as it is." He is also "pessimistic" about the human condition and moral ability.[30] Whiteside sensed that the deeper, more fundamental, issue with Boll was competing views of Christianity. For Whiteside Christianity focused upon human responsibility in restoring the church. Boll's theology gutted such an approach by acknowledging divine intervention.

Armstrong remained convinced that the "scare over 'Bollism'" was only a "scare-crow." Agreeing with G. C. Brewer that the issues were not worth discussing, he nonetheless preferred free discussion to mounting coercion. Thus he suggested "that R. L. Whiteside and R. H. Boll represent the two sides in the discussion. Whiteside has been called 'the brains of Texas' and is recognized as a man of superior ability....Boll, of course, is the man to represent his own contentions."[31]

Boll never made his understanding a test of fellowship. He did not wish for others to bind theirs on him. "It is every brother's privilege to test it by God's word and to accept or reject it according to his findings." Though refusing to force his views on anyone, Boll claimed "the right to teach my convictions."[32]

Armstrong was not able to hold back the tide in the Churches of

Christ. R. L. Whiteside was joined by Foy E. Wallace, Jr. in the battle against Boll. In 1934 Armstrong refused to cave to pressure from Wallace to disfellowship Boll as other college presidents had. But now the fight would also involve bitter attacks on Armstrong and Harding College by E. R. Harper.[33]

Armstrong, who refused to bow before the intimidating power of the U.S. government in World War I, also refused to be cowed into giving up his freedom to think and speak. To the bitter end he and Boll held on to the freedom bequeathed to them by the NBST.

FREE CHILDREN OF GOD

Freedom is an important motif in biblical faith. At the center of Christian faith is a God who is supremely free. Creation and all that lies within it flow from a free act of love by the triune God. At the heart of redemptive history is the freest person who ever walked the face of the earth, Jesus of Nazareth. Then there is the Spirit who blows like the wind, coming and going as he pleases. Human beings image God with the exercise of freedom.

Jesus is God's great Liberator. He promised his disciples that "you will know the truth, and the truth will set you free" (John 8:32). It is not empty rhetoric to which the Son calls us. Rather, "if the Son sets you free, you will be free indeed" (John 8:36). The task of Jesus was the restoration of freedom that had been lost in humanity's fall.

Freedom courses through the writings of Paul. The frequency of Greek words for freedom in Paul's writings—twenty-eight in all—indicate how important it was to him. "For whoever was called in the Lord as a slave is a freed person belonging to the Lord" (1 Cor 7:22). "Now the Lord is the Spirit, and where the Spirit is there is, there is freedom" (2 Cor 3:17).

F. F. Bruce calls Paul the "apostle of the heart set free."[34] Perhaps no Pauline letter makes the case for Christian freedom as brilliantly as Galatians. In the biblical story of freedom God is always the subject and humanity is the object. This is seen in the opening lines of Galatians. Paul is made an apostle by God. Jesus is raised from the dead by God. We are rescued from this evil age by God. We are acted upon before we respond. True freedom begins, then, in God's gracious deliverance. At its most basic level Christian freedom is freedom to live (cf. John 10:10).

Paul is adamant that any message that undercuts the free life in Christ by claiming God's work as our own is cursed (1:6-9). Paul is not attacking diversity in the body in Galatians 1. Rather he is attacking the idea that deliverance is a human achievement. Diversity was completely healthy and a sign of the Spirit himself (cf. 1 Cor 12:1-13).

There is no doubt, as Peterson has observed, that the Christian life is "a dancing, leaping, daring life."[35] It was this daring and adventurous life, with its freedom to adopt an entirely new perspective on reality, that some "false believers" (2:4) found disturbing. Paul notes that there are those who claim to be believers who actually infiltrate the ranks of disciples "to spy on the freedom we have in Christ Jesus and make us slaves" (2:4). No doubt these "false believers" had the best of motives. They wished to preserve morality in the face of paganism. They desired to protect the integrity of Scripture from compromise. But disciples, given life by God, are free to resist those who would make life in Christ even more burdensome than life outside Christ.

Perhaps the heart of Paul's defense of Christian freedom is rooted in Galatians 2:11-21. The apostle of freedom makes five statements that get to the heart of our relationship with the Father. These breathtaking assertions by Paul are the cogs that support a robust conception of freedom in Christ. Peter was gripped by fear of the false believers and withdrew from disciples who were not approved by that group (2:11-13). Paul boldly rebukes Peter before the entire assembly because he failed to realize that our standing before God was not a matter of right ritual, right company, or right tradition. By his action, Peter denied God's method of deliverance. We are justified, set free, made right by God, through faith in Christ (2:15-16).

When Paul states one truth it allows him to deny another that is fundamental to the false believers. Because justification is by faith it is not by "human effort" (3:3, NIV). Neither Peter, nor any other

Christian, has to be intimidated into a performance-based relationship with God. No amount of pressure from those who want to enslave will ever change the gospel of justification by faith in Christ. Disciples no longer have to try to impress God with false righteousness.

Paul's next statement is that we "ourselves are sinners" (2:17). This is the truth that many wish to hide. We deceive ourselves into thinking that we can faithfully meet God's righteous demands through our own moral prowess. But in light of God's great work through the cross we must admit our sinfulness. Claiming the title of "sinner" is not done out of pride but because we recognize that now we are objects of God's infinite mercy.

The apostle's claim of "sinner" was bold but his next claim is daring. Disciples are free because they have been "crucified with Christ" (2:20). The life of slavery has been abolished. Now because "Christ is your life" (Col 3:4) the Lord lives his own free life through us.

What makes this all possible, Paul claims, is the "grace of God" (2:20). Grace is the atmosphere the church breaths. The Christian life is God sharing his life with us. We do not attain a certain level of perfection. Paul tells the Galatians that to surrender their liberty by buying into false conceptions of our relationship with God is tantamount to saying that "Christ died for nothing!" (Gal 2:21).

So rich is God that he pours his Holy Spirit into our hearts to experience intimacy. "God sent the Spirit of his Son into our hearts who calls out, '*Abba*, Father'" (4:6). This was done because God has changed the nature of the relationship. The false believers still approached God as employees, slaves, or minors at best. But the Father has granted us the "full rights" of heirs (4:5). Thus, Paul exhorts his brothers and sisters: "It is for freedom that Christ has set us free. Stand firm, then and do not let yourselves be burdened again by a yoke of slavery" (5:1).

Because standing before God was a matter of grace rather than performance, Paul was able to exhibit great tolerance and patience with others. When his enemies stirred up trouble for him on his many missionary trips, he was able to thank God. Some preach Christ out of "false motives" and others "not sincerely." But it does not matter according to Paul. "The important thing is that in every way, whether from false motives or true, Christ is preached. And because of this I rejoice" (Phil 1:18). When his beloved coworkers, Euodia and Syntyche, could not agree with one another, he did not take sides. It did not even matter who was right or wrong, what mattered was that neither were exhibiting the attitude of Christ Jesus (Phil 4:2-3; 2:5-11).

Given his radical freedom in Christ, Paul found it wise to become all things to all people in order to win them to Christ. Thus, when he was with Gentiles he freely embraced their life. But when with his Jewish family he breathlessly claims the freedom to visit the temple, offer sacrifices, and even to pay for the sacrifices of others (Acts 21:17-26). No doubt Paul would defend his participation in such worship by saying that he did it "unto the Lord" (cf. Rom 14:5-8).

Freedom is not found in humanistic enterprises. Christian freedom does not establish the individual as an end to herself. We are not called to be free from God, his gracious Torah or restraint. Rather freedom calls us to adventuresome living for the sake of the kingdom. Jesus models freedom for the kingdom when he denied himself and took up the cross for the sake of redemption. Embracing the freedom Jesus models allows disciples to create space for brothers and sisters who do not agree with them in every detail (Rom 14-15). Freedom thus finds is fullest fulfillment in love.

ATTITUDES FOR EMBRACING GOD'S GIFT OF FREEDOM

Through the centuries many have found freedom a dangerous notion. Perhaps Albert Camus had this in mind when he stated in his Nobel Prize acceptance speech, "Liberty is dangerous, as hard to get along with as it is exciting."[36] To embrace liberty as a principle means we actively create space for those who, through their own study, come to conclusions different from our own. But such a posture is sound if we truly believe our relationship with God is grounded in his active grace toward us rather than on our grasp of doctrine, ritual or life.

Free to Think

The invitation of the Lord Jesus is an invitation to learn. We are called to a life-long journey of learning "of Jesus" (Matt 11:29). There may be millions of students but there is only one teacher. Whether we have been in the school of Jesus for one year or sixty years we never graduate. The word "disciple" describes who we are not just something we do. The longer we "learn of Jesus" the more we take on the characteristics of humility and gentleness.

As we follow Paul's counsel to "do your best to present yourself to God as one approved, a workman who does not need to be ashamed and who handles correctly the word of truth" (2 Tim 2:15), we realize that the profundity of the word is beyond our sophomoric abilities. God's word is always beyond our feeble interpretations of it. Thus, as we ponder the depths of God's word we cry for the Lord himself to be our teacher:

> Teach me, O LORD, to follow your decrees;
> then I will keep them to the end.
> Give me understanding, and I will keep your law
> and obey it with all my heart.
> Direct me in the path of your commands,
> for there I find delight. (Ps 119:33-35, NIV)

With the Lord teaching and directing our thinking we say with the psalmist, "I will walk in freedom" (Ps 119:45, NIV). We do not fall into the trap of the Pharisees in thinking that study of the word grants eternal life. Rather, we freely explore the word because it is a vehicle to relationship with Jesus (John 5:39-40).

Love for the word creates the freedom to think. But as the word settles into our hearts we are conscious that it is handled inappropriately, as Paul states, when we use it as a weapon to fight each other. Satan loves it when we fight over "words" (2 Tim 2:14) because that turns the word into an object we control. Boll testified in the heat of the premillennial battle that many "were intensely occupied with words" yet fail to "see the Word." The scriptures are analogous to an engraving he had seen of the Constitution. The artist had skillfully etched the plate so that when held a short distance from the eyes there appeared a portrait of George Washington in the midst of the words. "Thus is the face of Jesus" revealed in the Scriptures. Those who can pick about for "doctrinal or controversial points" and yet miss the "vision of truth and love in the face of Jesus Christ" have a knowledge that is after the "letter" but not the Spirit.[37] But with the Lord as the teacher we learn humility and gentleness with one another, even as we probe the riches. As we search "the Lord will give [us] understanding in all things" (2 Tim 2:7).

Freedom to Fail

It sounds like an oxymoron at first. Those who conceive of Christianity as fulfilling a law code will not accept it. R. H. Boll observed that this view "is altogether a wrong attitude, productive of miserable, forced service...such a man is a bond servant not a son." These neurotic disciples are "constantly haunted by fear" that they are "not sufficiently holy to procure the favor of God."[38]

Yet if we believe that our relationship is rooted in the grace of God and the blood of Christ then Christians are free to fail. We do not seek failure. But we rest secure knowing that failure does not sever saints from relationship with God. On the contrary we "stand" by grace (Rom 5:2). Even though we sin there is no condemnation for those who are in Christ Jesus (Rom 8:1). The man with the single talent was not condemned because he failed. He was condemned because he was afraid to take a risk for the master and did nothing at all (Matt 25:24-27). Peter's failure to act properly in Galatia did not consign him to hell, nor did it disqualify him from future service to the family of God.

Knowing that God still holds us tight, despite our failure, is a powerful impetus to delve even deeper into the wells of God's word and serve him. We will never have every passage understood perfectly. Paul testifies that there were some Corinthian disciples whose understanding of the faith was so shallow that some still held onto polytheism (1

Cor 8:7). These babes knew just enough to believe in the gospel of Christ crucified, and therefore Paul argued that love was more important than knowledge in dealing with them (1 Cor 8:1-2).

Based on God's gift to us, we extend it to others. We allow others to grow, think, and make mistakes. Like Paul with the Corinthians we are only called to live by what we know. Speaking to the Philippians Paul makes the following incredible statement: "Let those of us then who are mature be of the same mind; and if you think differently about anything, this too God will reveal to you. Only let us hold fast to what we have attained" (3:15-16).

What an incredible apostolic example Paul left for us!

Free to Love and Fellowship

The example of Paul with his churches and the courage of Armstrong testify that we are free to love and free to fellowship those with whom we disagree. It was the apostle's example that had forced Alexander Campbell to overcome his narrow exclusiveness. "I was once so strict a Separatist," Campbell lamented, "that I would neither pray nor sing praises with any one who was not as perfect as I supposed myself."[39] Campbell came to recognize the different paths he had taken and the one taken by Paul. If Paul could fellowship a congregation that was as full of error as the Corinthians, Campbell wondered why he could not.

Perhaps it is no accident that the community most affected by the world around it, the church that was rife with division, the people who were plagued with worship chaos, the assembly that even had folks who denied the resurrection, was the very congregation to receive the greatest meditation on love ever written. Despite their acknowledged problems, the Corinthians had embraced the Christ of God and were God's family. Thus Paul, even in light of all their issues, "always thank[ed] God for [them] because of his grace given [them] in Christ Jesus" (1 Cor 1:4). The Corinthians' failure, like Peter's, did not disqualify them from being part of God's redeemed community.

Love is the spiritual gift that holds the community together in this hostile age. Love is patient with another student's apparent lack of understanding. Love keeps no records of the failings of those in the community. Love rejoices in all truth discovered. Love is more important than correct knowledge. A community so defective as the one at Corinth was still fully embraced by God and his apostle because of divine love. This is a model we are called to emulate.

CONCLUSION

Freedom to think and speak was an integral part of the NBST. This does not mean its leaders never drew the line in the sand, because that is clearly not the case. Yet the leaders of this rich theological tradition in Churches of Christ were convinced that it was only through the freedom to think and speak that the community as a whole moved to a greater understanding of God's holy will. Freedom was also the answer to Christ's prayer for unity in John 17. It is a bold legacy that has been passed down to us. Imagine the renewal that could take place in our congregations when we embrace the freedom to think, the freedom to fail, and the freedom to love and fellowship. Claiming such freedom places us in hallowed company.

DISCUSSION QUESTIONS

1. How can the Armstrong/Boll affair be characterized as a "quest" for freedom? What has been your experiences relating to the freedom to think and speak? Is freedom in Christ suppressed in our churches? How is freedom balanced with obligation to the community of faith?

2. How does the doctrine of grace establish an atmosphere conducive to freedom? How does the idea of being a student relate to judging other disciples?

3. Does Paul's example of freedom to love and fellowship the Corinthians serve as a model for contemporary churches?

CHALLENGES

Find a way to open channels of communication in your congregation for dissenting voices to be heard.

Seek out an estranged member of the family of God and extend the grace of fellowship

PRAYER

Father, we praise you for the freedom you have granted us as your children. We are often, Father, afraid of freedom because of its unpredictability. Grant us courage to live as freely as our brother Jesus. Father, because of our own lack of courage, we sometimes try to restrict the freedom of our brother or our sister. We need your magnanimous Spirit to refrain from judging. Fill us with an adventurous sense of freedom so we can explore the limitless dimensions of our relationship with you. Amen.

RESOURCES

Eugene Peterson, *Traveling Light: Modern Meditations on St. Paul's Letter of Freedom* (Colorado Springs: Helmers & Howard, 1988)

Jack R. Reese, *The Broken Body: Embracing the Peace of Christ in A Fragmented World* (Siloam Springs, AR: Leafwood, 2005)

ELEVEN

SHADOWS NO MORE: TOWARD COSMIC LIBERATION

...the earth is God's nursery, his training grounds, made primarily for the occupancy of his children, for their education, development and training until they shall have reached their majority, until the end of the Messianic age has come; then it is to be purified a second time by a great washing, a mighty flood, but this time in a sea of fire. Then God will take up his abode himself with his great family upon this new, this renovated and purified earth...So it is apparent that the one great, all-including purpose for which we were made, for which we exist, is to be educated, trained, developed, so as to be indeed sons of God; brothers of Christ, heirs of God, who will dwell with their Father forever, and will reign with him.

—James A. Harding (1903) [1]

In the 1920s and 1930s, premillennialism became a divisive topic among Churches of Christ.[2] Up to that time, premillennial perspectives had been taught and tolerated. Barton W. Stone, Moses Lard, T. W. Brents and many others were premillennialists.[3] By the 1930s, however, some premillennialists (such as Boll) had moved solidly into the ranks of Dispensationalists, and anti-premillennialists (such as Whiteside) had rejected any kind of apocalyptic vision by strictly equating the church and the kingdom. The exclusion of premillennalism (even the historic version of Lard and Brents) from Churches of Christ coincided with the practical death of the "apocalyptic" worldview among them.

Though Harding was a premillennialist,[4] premillennialism was not the substance of his kingdom vision. Many, including Armstrong and Boll, held premillennial beliefs (e.g., that Jesus would reign a thousand years on the earth prior to the new heavens and new earth), but this was not the heart of their eschatology. Lipscomb himself was agnostic on premillennialism.[5] The more fundamental premise was new creation, that is, God will renew this earth as a home of the righteous and reign upon it forever. The kingdom of God, conceived as the progressive reign of God ultimately restoring the cosmos under the full rule of God, is the structural principle of NBST eschatology. As R. C. Bell—one-time student at the NBS and teacher at PBS—commented, Harding's understanding of Christianity was "built upon an eschatological framework."[6] Eschatology is the engine that drove salvation history in the NBST.

The central story is how God progressively introduced his reign into the world so as to reclaim his dominion—first through Israel, then in the ministry of Jesus, and then through the church. While the millennial reign of Christ for Harding was a further introduction of that progressive reign within redemptive history, it was not the final stage. Rather, the Father would himself come to dwell with his people in a new heaven and new earth, a new creation. There not only humanity, but the cosmos itself would be liberated from the bondage of sin and death. This is the goal of God's redemptive project. Lipscomb and Harding, along with Alexander Campbell, Tolbert Fanning and Robert Milligan among others, believed that God would reign with his people on a renewed earth forever. When Jesus returns "again to earth," according to Lipscomb, he will accomplish the "restoration of all things to their original relation to God" in a new heaven and new earth.[7] Then God the Father will rule "through his restored kingdom on earth" and will "be all and in all, the only ruler of the heavens and of the earth."[8]

HARDING'S ESCHATOLOGICAL TRAJECTORY

God created the cosmos for the "purpose of enlarging the family of God." God, as a triune community, graciously decided to create others who would share the divine fellowship. God wanted to add "a great host of 'sons of God'" to his family—people made "after the likeness of God" who would be "educated, trained and fitted to reign with Christ as members of the royal family, as children of the King."[9] God created humanity "to rule his universe," and thus gave it the dignity of "his own image, and began at once to train [humanity] in ruling."[10] God created the world and put it into the hands of his vice-regents while they were yet in "pristine purity."[11]

However, God's vice-regents quickly turned creation "over to Satan." The Fall introduced the struggle between good and evil in the creation. But God soon destroyed the wicked and renewed his creation through the Noahic flood. "God swept Satan's servants from the face of the earth, and again gave it to the righteous" in the days of Noah, but "they turned it over to Satan again." The struggle continues even now. "The war is raging, the war of righteousness against wickedness, of Christ against Satan, of the kingdom of heaven, under the leadership of Jesus, against the kingdoms of this world, under the leadership of Satan."[12] This dualism dominates Harding's theology and it is the fundamental ground for his sense that the church is a community of resident aliens in the fallen world.

Throughout this struggle, God is present with his people as he educates, matures and trains them for their future role in the new heaven and new earth. In a key article, Harding laid out a redemptive-historical understanding of this presence.[13] He unfolds the progressive nature of God's presence. Israel experienced God's presence through the tabernacle and temple where an angel was "God's representative on earth" (cf. Exodus 23:20-23; 32:34). Then God himself dwelt among us as the incarnate Son. Jesus was "Immanuel." In this sense, God was "with" his people and the Spirit was also "with" them in the ministry of Jesus (cf. John 14:17).

However, something decisive happened at Pentecost that introduced a new era. It is the "peculiarity of the new covenant" that God now dwells "in" his people through his Spirit. This was the promise of John 7:37-39 fulfilled on Pentecost when God poured out his Spirit and indwelt his people. God the Father still has a representative on earth. But unlike his angelic presence with Israel, or the Son's incarnational presence, now God dwells *in* his people. God and Christ dwell representatively through the personal presence of the Holy Spirit (Eph 2:22). Thus, "as in former dispensations God dwelt among his people, so does he now; then, in the presence of an angel, now, in the presence of the Holy Spirit;" then "with" his people, now "in" his people.[14]

Yet, even this is not the final stage of God's redemption. Just as "a greater age, a greater people and a greater temple required a greater representative from the Celestial City"[15]—and we now have that by the presence of the Spirit in the church, God's temple—so we anticipate a fuller presence of God in the new heaven and the new earth.

Harding's theology of the Spirit, then, is partly a function of his eschatological structure. Now the Holy Spirit dwells within the church in the present stage of redemptive history. The millennial reign is the time when Christ will return to dwell among his people, and the new heaven and new earth will be the time when the Father himself returns to Eden upon a renewed earth. The history of redemption is the history of God's progressive presence among his people to restore them to Eden and thus fulfill his original intent in creation.

The "Messianic age" is the time when God revealed his kingdom in Jesus Christ. "The beginning of Christ's reign was announced on earth on the first Pentecost after his resurrection." It now continues through the church as the kingdom is advanced through its ministry, and it will culminate in Christ's return to the earth where he will reign for a thousand years. "From all this it is evident that the last thousand years of Christ's reign will be a period of perfect rest from sin."[16] Eden will return and fulfill God's original purpose in creation. Humanity will reign again upon the earth—first with Christ in the millennium and then with the Father in the new heaven and new earth.[17]

Harding's second advent scenario included these elements. At present the kingdom of Christ and the kingdom of Satan are engaged in a war for the hearts of people. Satan "dwells on the earth" to deceive the nations and devour Christians.[18] However, Christ will come again to destroy the works of Satan and fully establish his kingdom. He will come, raise the dead and rapture the saints with their immortal bodies. "When the saints are caught up to meet him, Christ comes on with them to the earth."[19] The kings of the earth will gather to do battle under the leadership of the beast, false prophet and Satan, and Christ will destroy them. While the false prophet and beast, along with the rest of the wicked on the earth are destroyed, Satan is chained and thrown into the abyss. While Satan is bound, "Christ and his saints reign; but the rest of the dead live not again till the thousand years have expired."[20] During this "last thousand years of time, Christ and his saints shall reign unimpeded in the earth. Then the meek shall inherit the earth, the knowledge of God shall fill the earth as the waters fill the seas, and the will of God shall be done on earth as it is in heaven."[21]

This millennial reign "on the earth" is the "Sabbath rest" for all the people of God and the earth.[22] According to Harding, the "seventh day was typical of the Sabbath rest that awaits the people of God when for a thousand years they shall rest from sin, temptation, pain and sorrow."[23] Since the earth labored and groaned for six thousand years under the burden of fallenness, according to Harding, the millennial reign is a rest for the earth as well as for God's people.

The millennial reign of Christ on earth will near its end when Satan is released from the abyss to "deceive the nations that are in the four corners of the earth."[24] Demonic spirits will gather to do battle with Christ and his saints, and after their defeat the judgment will follow. The earth will be purged by fire and Satan thrown into hell. The righteous will reign with God on the "new earth."[25]

The new heaven and the new earth then appear. This is the reign of the Father to whom the Son will turn over the kingdom.[26] The millennial reign of Christ is not the end of the story but anticipates the next "great epoch in the history of God's dealing with" humanity.[27] While the Sabbath typifies the millennial reign of Christ, the "first day of the week foreshadows the glories of beginning a new life in the everlasting kingdom of God."[28] This new heaven and new earth with its new Jerusalem is not some celestial city, but is itself the kingdom of God on the purified earth. In this way God's intent in creation to have children reign with him over the earth is accomplished.

CREATED FOR THE KINGDOM

God created a community among whom he could dwell. Humanity was created in the image of God to share God's benevolent rule over the earth. We were tasked to "take care of" (serve) the earth (Gen 2:15) and to image the God who loves, rejoices over, delights in and wisely serves the cosmos (cf. Ps 104; Job 38-39). God created cosmic *shalom* and graciously invited humanity to serve with him as co-regents over it. And God saw that it was "very good" (Gen 1:31).

But the creation was overcome by crisis as humanity created an alternative story. Adam and Eve sought autonomy at the forbidden tree (Gen 3), Cain committed fratricide (Genesis 4), death became the final tally in human lineages (Gen 5), the whole earth imagined evil in the days of Noah (Gen 6-9), and ultimately human arrogance asserted equality with God ("let us build...a tower that reaches to the heavens" and "make a name for ourselves," Gen 11:4). Humanity introduced a different trajectory into God's good creation, but it was a degenerative path. It vandalized the *shalom* of Eden and introduced hostility between male and female, between human communities, and between humanity and nature. The good creation was turned upside down.

Nevertheless, God pursued us. In response to Cain's violence, God gave life through the birth of Seth. Even though death enslaved humanity, Enoch walked with God and escaped death. Though destroying the earth because of its sin, God preserved the earth and humanity for the hope of a new beginning through Noah's descendents. And rather than swallowing up the builders of Babel, God scattered them so that the whole earth would be inhabited (cf. Isa 45:18). While God's response to the degenerative process of Genesis 3-11 certainly included punishment that served God's goal of redeeming creation, at the same time God's grace pursued humanity. The creation still remained and God yearned for a renewal of communion with his imagers. God still wanted to dwell with his people.

God's intent to dwell with his people is a pervasive theme in Scripture. When God entered into the covenant of circumcision, he promised that Abraham's descendants would be his people and he would be their God (Gen 17:7-8). When God came to Israel in Egypt through Moses, he assured them that "I will take you as my own people, and I will be your God" (Ex 6:7). When Israel set up the tabernacle in the wilderness, God's glory descended upon it (Ex 29:45; 40:34-35; Lev 26:11-12). God's presence came again with the completion of the temple under Solomon (1 Kgs 8:11; 2 Chr 5:14; 7:1-3). The prophets constantly reminded the people of God's promise to be present among them (Ezek. 34:30). Israel is God's people and Yahweh is their God (Jer 7:23; 11:4; 24:7; Ezek 11:20; 14:11; 36:28; 37:27; Zech 2:11; 8:8; 13:9).

This promise was at the heart of the "new covenant." Though Israel was unfaithful, God declared his intent to forgive their sin and give them a heart of obedience so that he could fulfill his promise among them—"I will be their God and they will be my people" (Jer 31:33). Paul, thinking about the ministry of this new covenant (2 Cor 3:6), reminds us that this promise is given to the church since "we are the temple of the living God" (2 Cor 6:16). This means that Leviticus 26:11-12 has been fulfilled, as God has said: "I will live with them and walk among them, and I will be their God, and they will be my people" (2 Cor 6:16 quoting Lev). But this promise is ultimately fulfilled in the eschatological dwelling of God with his people when the new age is consummated. When the new Jerusalem descends out of heaven, then a loud voice will announce: "Now the dwelling of God is with men, and he will live with them. They will be his people, and God himself will be with them and be their God" (Rev 21:3).

This redemptive-historical plot demonstrates that God's intent in redemption/recreation is to dwell with his people in a communion of love. This communion, however, is not apart from the created cosmos.

God redeems (renews) his creation as a new heaven and new earth. God's redemptive pursuit is cosmic in character. He seeks fellowship with his people on the earth.

God will redeem creation itself, just as he will redeem our bodies (Rom 8:23). He will turn everything back to its original purpose, both things on the earth and things in heaven (Col 1:20). Just as he will redeem fallen bodies through resurrection, so he will redeem the fallen creation through recreation even as he now transforms our inner persons through his Holy Spirit.

According to Romans 8:19-23, the creation, including our bodies, was subjected to the futility and bondage of a fallen world. God subjected the world to frustration in the hope of liberating the creation from its bondage. This world, full of its sin, violence and disease, is not the world God created. God's good creation has been marred, but his redemptive intent is to renew it. God will create a new heaven and a new earth (Rev 21:1-4; 2 Pet 3:13; cf. Isa 65:17; 66:22) where he will dwell among humankind in a new city, in a new Garden of Eden. There will be no more pain, no more tears, and no more death (Rev 21:1-4; 22:1-5). There will be no more curse. God will fulfill the intention he had from the beginning. In the end, God will reverse the curse and renew the earth, living among his people just as he did in the Garden.

Sometimes our view of heaven is too other-worldly. We think that heaven is some ethereal, almost surreal, place somewhere in the sky. We think heaven is out-there, over-there, or somewhere other than here. Certainly, here and now is not heaven—it is far from it. This place is full of violence, death, hostility, tears and pain. But this is not what God created. He created Eden where harmony, peace and joy reigned; and where God communed with his newly created human community. One day, God will destroy the fallenness that envelops the present earth and renew it so that it might be inhabited by his saints.

Anthony Hokema rejects the total annihilation of the old heaven and earth in favor of a renewed one for four basic reasons.[29] First, the newness of the heavens and the earth (2 Pet 3:13; Rev 21:1) is described by *kainos* (new in quality or nature) rather than *neos* (new in time or origin). Something old is given a new quality rather than creating a whole new reality out of nothing. Second, Romans 8 teaches that the material earth will be redeemed along with our own material bodies. Third, the analogy between our resurrected bodies and the new earth points in the direction of materiality. While there will be discontinuity between the old and new earths, there will be also be, just like with the resurrection body, continuity between the old and new earths. Fourth, "if God would have to annihilate the present cosmos, Satan would have won a great victory." Has Satan so corrupted this world that it must be annihilated and a new one erected? Did God lose the battle for this earth? On the contrary, God's victory is decisive and complete—he will redeem the earth he created.

Our hope, then, is to reign with God on the earth. Our hope is the restoration of God's good creation. The old heaven and the old earth will be purified by fire and renewed for inhabitation by God's saints (2 Pet 3:10-13).[30] Perhaps this makes more sense of certain biblical phrases like, "the meek shall inherit the earth" (Matthew 5:5; cf. Ps 37:11), or that Gentiles, as part of the promise of Abraham, would inherit the cosmos (Rom 4:13).[31] The meaning of the new heaven and the new earth is that God will redeem the cosmos—everything in heaven and earth will be reconciled to him again. God will turn the world back upright. Everything will be made new, Eden will be restored, and there will no longer be any curse (Rev 22:1-5). In the restored tranquility of the Garden—a garden that will fill the earth—we will reign with God forever and live in *shalom* with each other and the cosmos. Then, as Lipscomb said, "earth itself will become heaven."[32]

KINGDOM HOPE AND LIVING

God intends to dwell among his people on the earth and even now is at work to reverse the effects of the fall through the presence of his kingdom. This promise not only grounds fallen humanity's hope, but empowers them to participate in God's redemptive purpose in the present.

Hope for the Future

Believers yearn for the revelation of their glorious freedom as the children of God. Paul calls this the "groaning" of the believers (Rom 8:23). It is a groan that arises out of the expectation of something new, something redemptive. We groan for the consummation because we are perplexed, struck down and persecuted by the fallen world even though we are not crushed, despairing or destroyed because of hope (2 Cor 4:7-9). But hope generates a groan or a yearning because we do not yet have that for which we hope. The indwelling Spirit is God's down payment on eschatological glory (2 Cor 1:22; 5:5; Eph 1:14). This presence is the presence of the future in our hearts so that we are emboldened with hope for the future. We experience hope by the power of the Spirit (Rom 8:24-25; 15:13).

The Spirit of God actively works on behalf of the God's people through their prayers. The Spirit, Paul writes, "helps us in our weaknesses" (Rom 8:26). In the immediate context, Paul is thinking about prayer. But the Spirit is not far from Paul's mind when he thinks about suffering, groaning and hope. As he turns from the present suffering to a sense of the "already," the Spirit is uppermost in his mind. The presence of the Spirit is an "already." We wait in the power of the Spirit as we groan for the "not yet." Fallenness remains as the *eschaton* has "not yet" come. In our fallen state, we experience weakness and need the help of God's Spirit. Even in our praying—our most desperate attempt to seek God's face—we are weak and need help. The Spirit is present to aid our weaknesses and that weakness is overcome by God's power through prayer.

Through prayer the Spirit intercedes for us. Intimacy is assumed here. The Spirit knows our hearts and because he knows us so well, he is able to intercede for us. The Spirit is the relational dynamic that connects us with God. God knows the mind of the Spirit just as the Spirit knows our inexpressible groanings as he himself groans for us. This is the language of intimacy, fellowship and shared experience. The Spirit suffers with us, just as God suffered with Israel in the Old Testament and Jesus suffered with us incarnationally. Now the Spirit too suffers with us and shares this experience with the Father in ways that words cannot describe. Through the shared experience of suffering and groaning, the eschatological Spirit produces hope in our hearts.

Hastening the Future

Harding and Boll lived with a fervent expectancy of the second coming. Noting the many natural disasters of the previous fifty years (including thousands killed by volcanoes and earthquakes), Harding spoke of the "signs of His second coming" and that "for the last fifty or sixty years many godly men have believed that the time of his coming is near." Believers, if they read the signs, will not be surprised by his coming, though he comes as a thief in the night for those who are not watching. Believers should be "ready." And readiness means not only "watching," but living—to "live for" the coming of the "everlasting kingdom."[33] This entails a total reorientation of our lifestyle. We live as if the kingdom has arrived and in expectation of its imminent arrival.

> We would not be as eager about laying up supplies for the future as most people are, but we would rather be eager to do all the good possible. We would read the Bible more, pray more, attend church more; we would be anxious to minister to the poor, the sick, the aged, the oppressed; we would be more eager to give than to receive…we would be gentler, kinder, more sympathetic.[34]

This kind of living is a cry for the kingdom. It lives the kingdom in the present even as it yearns for the full reality of the kingdom. Indeed, it "hastens" the coming of the kingdom. Based on the language of 2 Peter 3:12 ("waiting and hastening the coming of the day"), Boll emphasized that kingdom living sped the coming of God as the world was increasingly filled with the presence of the kingdom through the lives of kingdom disciples.[35]

The mission of the kingdom is to redeem fallenness. If the church is an outpost of the kingdom, and the kingdom is present in the world through the church, then the mission of the church is to redeem poverty, social injustice and ecology. The mission of the church is beyond "saving souls" in some spiritualized sense. It includes a proclamation of forgiveness, but salvation is more than forgiveness. It is wholeness; it is the restoration of *shalom* and the reconciliation of all the hostile forces in the world.

We cry for the kingdom by participating in the kingdom agenda. We are involved in a great reclamation project. We seek to reclaim the cosmos for God and be instruments of his reign in the world. This is the essence of the kingdom—to reverse the curse. As doctors and nurses, we seek to reverse the curse of disease, sickness and death. As educators, we seek to reverse the curse of deforming ignorance and empower students to participate in the mission of the kingdom. As counselors, we seek ways to reverse the breakdown in relationships within families. As bankers and economists, we seek ways to reverse poverty. As environmentalists, we serve the cosmos as stewards of God's good creation and seek to reverse the pollution of the earth.

To proclaim the good news of the kingdom is to become world-involving. We participate in reclaiming the cosmos for God—we reclaim economics, social justice, and ecology for God. We reclaim forgiveness over guilt, health over sickness, and provision over impoverishment. We reclaim the marginalized and disenfranchised in a community of reconciliation. The mission of Jesus is the mission of the church—to proclaim good news to the "poor." It is God's mission to reclaim the "poor" (the cursed) for himself and renew his earth with *shalom*—peace between God and humanity, between human communities, and between humanity and the cosmos (cf. Ps 146; Isa 61:1-3; Luke 4:14-30). This is the mission of the kingdom, and it is the essence of kingdom living.

Eschatology not only provides hope for the future, but also empowers mission for the present. It brings the goal of God—the future of God—into the present. The mission of the church is to reverse the curse so as to hasten the future.

CONCLUSION

Believers are caught between the "not yet" of fallenness and the "already" of the *eschaton*. This tension means that we live in two worlds. We live in the futility of suffering, death, mourning, alienation, violence and pain, but we also live in the Spirit who gives hope, peace and comfort. We are oppressed by the world's fallenness, but we are liberated and renewed by the indwelling Spirit. This tension creates the situation where believers must wait for something they already partially possess. Believers wait for the eschaton with a hope that overcomes the futility of fallenness.

But this hope is no "pie in the sky in the bye and bye." Rather, this hope is the presence of the future that transforms the present. By the power of the Spirit, the future kingdom of God is already present in our lives to equip and empower us to participate in the present reality of the kingdom. We live in certain hope of the future in such a way that we live as if the kingdom of God has already arrived. We are free to serve in the kingdom as we wait for full cosmic liberating power of the kingdom. This is God's world and he will win it back.

This is my Father's World
O let me ne'er forget
That though the wrong seems oft so strong
God is the ruler yet.

This is my Father's world!
The battle is not done;
Jesus who died shall be satisfied
And earth and heav'n be one.[36]

DISCUSSION QUESTIONS

1. How does Harding's understanding of the kingdom connect with your own? How is it different or the same? What aspects of his description resonate with you?

2. What is the meaning of "new creation"—for the present as well as the future? How does the NBST vision of a "new earth" affect how we act presently in relation to our bodies, the environment, etc.? How does it enlarge our vision of "salvation"?

3. How does your occupation serve the kingdom agenda to reverse the curse? In what ways does your job participate in the kingdom of God?

CHALLENGES

Identify one dimension of your occupation that you can transform so that people can see the reality of the future kingdom in your present work environment.

Identify a curse that God has gifted you to reverse this week and proactively pursue God's kingdom agenda on that point.

PRAYER

Our heavenly Father, we cry for the kingdom. Bring your kingdom into the present and transform this world into your new creation. May your will be don on earth as it is heaven. May the earth be filled with your righteousness and peace. Father, make us instruments of your peace this day. Lord, come quickly. Amen.

SUGGESTED READING

Albert M. Wolters, *Creation Regained: Biblical Basis for a Reformational Worldview* (Grand Rapids: Eerdmans, 1985).

Ben Witherington, III, *Jesus, Paul and the End of the World: A Comparative Study in New Testament Eschatology* (Downers Grove, IL: InterVarsity, 1992).

Randy Alcorn, *Heaven* (Wheaton: Tyndale House Publishers, 2004).

Michael E. Wittmer, *Heaven Is a Place on Earth* (Grand Rapids: Zondervan, 2004).

TWELVE

THE ROAD NOT TRAVELED: WHERE DO WE GO FROM HERE?

Has Christianity collapsed, and the gospel proved a failure? No! The foundation of the Lord stands….The nations and kingdoms of this world are not His. They know it and He knows it. But the elect of every nation…are his.
—Robert H. Boll (1916)[1]

We began our journey by asking the question if anything good could come out of 1906. We hope this book is evidence that there are precious diamonds from that period that shine even brighter because of the clouds of division. The NBST provided a rich alternative to the paths in the Disciples of Christ and the Texas Tradition—both of which, at times, appealed in their own way to the self-sufficiency of humanity.

But what happened to the jewels from those early years of the twentieth century? Obviously, many of the unique emphases of the NBST have not characterized the Churches of Christ. Indeed, many of the countercultural themes of Lipscomb and Harding are quite foreign to us in our American setting. How is it that we who have desired above all else to pattern ourselves after the life and practice of the first churches end up looking so western, so modern, and so American.

Some have even suggested that we became a "worldly church."[2] What are the reasons that our fellowship failed to travel down the kingdom road that Lipscomb and Harding sought to pave?

Perhaps the most important reason for the demise of the NBST was the decline and death of these two giants of faith. We might even be able to narrow this even further and place the downturn with the decline of Harding's health. Harding was the engine that drove the NBST. Lipscomb wrote brilliantly for the *Advocate* but Harding was the sought-out teacher and evangelist. He was the promoter of a vision that captured the hearts of thousands. His magnetic personality is what drew students first to Nashville and then to Bowling Green. Lipscomb, while always respected, did not have the same impact upon his students that Harding did. Harding lived and breathed the themes of this book and nurtured them in his students. The tradition was highly dependent upon Harding. There was not a person in the Churches of Christ who commanded the respect and attention of Harding to keep this tradition from being overshadowed. Many of his students, like Armstrong and Boll, did pass on this dynamic tradition, but for various reasons they could not replace the leadership of Harding.

Part of the problem can be laid at the feet of Lipscomb and Harding themselves. They diverted resources and energy from this grand kingdom theme to the divisive fights of the late 1880s-1910s over innovations (e.g., instrumental music and missionary socieities). Sometimes the kingdom vision was pushed into the background as more personal, congregational and hermeneutical issues overwhelmed the moment. As the church focused on in-fighting, it lost the overarching vision of the kingdom's in-breaking.

There were also other factors already in play before Lipscomb and Harding ended their public life. Within their lifetime pressure was mounting to back away from many of the positions associated with the NBST. J. C. Holloway and L. S. White attacked Harding's theology of the Holy Spirit and special providence and revealed an undercurrent that was moving toward common sense rationalism. The seeds for this assault upon the NBST lie in the Enlightenment presuppositions that undergird every branch of the Stone-Campbell Movement. The upsurge of the scientific worldview, the rise of nationalism, and the quest for an identity distinct from the Disciples were factors that drove the unique perspectives of Lipscomb and Harding to the fringes.

Richard Hughes has suggested that the Stone-Campbell Movement, and Churches of Christ in particular, embraced Campbellian rationalism rather than Stoneite apocalypticism in the 1830s.[3] Leonard Allen has suggested that in the 1850s-60s the Stone-Campbell Movement, and Churches of Christ in particular, chose Tolbert Fanning's Baconian rationalism over Robert Richardson's openness to the work of the Spirit beyond the sacred page.[4] Lipscomb and Harding, while certainly reflecting some aspects of this scientific rationalism (e.g., a command, example, inference hermeneutic concerning church practices), did not fully buy into the modern rationalism that dominated some quarters of the Stone-Campbell Movement. They chose a different path.

Their choice, however, met with opposition from within. The *Firm Foundation* (begun in 1884) opposed Lipscomb and eventually Harding on several fronts. This opposition, solidly located in Texas, grew in support in the Midwest (Ohio, Indiana, Illinois) and influenced others in the South as well. After the death of Lipscomb, Harding, Larimore, McQuiddy and others, Texas came to Tennessee. Foy E. Wallace, Jr. was appointed editor of the *Gospel Advocate* in 1930 and the rising voice in the east sounded Texan rather than Tennessean. Southern Churches of Christ who read the *Firm Foundation* and *Gospel* Advocate in the 1940s and 1950s generally heard the rational voice of common sense Baconianism rather than the "apocalyptic" kingdom language of Lipscomb and Harding.[5] The Texas Tradition had supplanted the Nashville Bible School Tradition. We believe that was a wrong turn in our history.

One of the clarion desires of our postmodern world is the desire for authenticity. This is also one of the impulses of the Churches of Christ. The world has watched as the church has accommodated to cultural values and judged it inauthentic. Institutional factors like *a cap-*

pella music, a sign that says "Church of Christ," and the exclusion of women from any visible presence in the assembly have been judged irrelevant to a meaningful life and discipleship. We do not think these matters insignificant but we do believe that perhaps our critics have a valid point—these "marks" do not come close to making us authentic disciples of Christ. The NBST challenges our present situation with this call for authenticity. The marks of authentic disciples are the values of the subversive kingdom of God. The NBST challenges us to be in the world but not of the world. It challenges us to be a city on the hill that cannot be hid and leaven in the world for the sake of the kingdom.

The NBST challenges us to live in and by the counterworld envisioned by Scripture.[6] We believe the NBST challenges us with a biblical spirituality that is at once both personal and communal. It is a spirituality that calls us to look at our "inner" life and care for the world around us. Perhaps we can call it an incarnational spirituality.

By returning to 1906 we discover that there was sin enough to go around. There were personalities and hidden agendas that even the participants failed to discern. But we listen to the past so that we are able to see our way into the future with greater clarity.[7]

Because we love God's church we take seriously its history. Just like the history recorded of our fathers and mothers in the Old Testament, it is a tale of tragedy and triumph. David was great and tragic, as was Hezekiah. So too are Lipscomb, Harding, Armstrong and Boll. The NBST is a frail human tradition—a human attempt to read and live Scripture, and it had its faults.

But their lives are also beacons in the storm that can help us see our way to living in the shadow of the coming kingdom of God. They illuminate a path that allows us to be true to the best of our heritage, true to the God we believe is working in and through, and to point nonbelievers to a way of life that images the restoration of God's promised *shalom* on earth. We are called to participate in a truly rich pilgrimage of faith in the coming kingdom. On that caravan route we find not only Lipscomb, Harding and Boll, but Abraham, Isaac, Jacob, Peter and Paul. Most significantly, it is a path that follows Jesus into the future kingdom of God.

Father of the holy family, we lament and confess our faithlessness in your coming kingdom, but we believe that you kingdom is coming. We pledge, henceforth, to live as resident aliens in this hostile world. We seek your power through your Spirit to witness to the transcendent kingdom of your presence. We pray not only for ourselves but for the family that bears your name. We pray, Abba, that your kingdom come so that your will may done on earth just as it is heaven. Amen.

NOTES

CHAPTER ONE: INTRODUCING A SPIRITUAL LEGACY

1 On this "third way," see C. Leonard Allen, *Things Unseen: Churches of Christ In (and After) the Modern Age* (Siloam Springs, AR: Leafwood Publishers, 2004), 133-152.

2 We, of course, do not mean that the influence of this tradition was restricted to Texas or that it was only present in Texas. This is not primarily a geographical description but a theological one. "Texas" is appropriate because the development and spread of these ideas was primarily—though not exclusively—associated with the *Firm Foundation*. This does not mean, of course, that everyone in Texas would have concurred with this tradition.

3 Cf. J. N. Armstrong, "Who and What We Are," *GH* 1 (31 October 1912), 4; R. L. Whiteside and N. L. Clark, *Whiteside-Clark Discussion* (Denton, Texas: Inys Whiteside Publisher, 1969), 5; and C. R. Nichol, *Gospel Preachers Who Blazed the Trail* (Austin, TX: Firm Foundation, 1911), cv. Whiteside (no pagination in original). Armstrong also called Whiteside the "brains of Texas" ("Remarks," *LM* 3 [23 July 1925], 468).

4 Robert P. Valentine, Jr., *Robertson Lafayette Whiteside: Systematic Theologian for the Churches of Christ* (unpublished Guided Research Paper, Harding University Graduate School of Religion, 2001).

5 Robertson L. Whiteside, *A New Commentary on Paul's Letter to the Saints at Rome* (Clifton, TX: Published by Mrs. C. R. Nichol, 1945) and with C. R. Nichol, *Sound Doctrine: A Series of Bible Studies for Sunday School Classes, Prayer Meetings, Private Studies, College Classes, etc.*, 5 volumes, 6th edition (Abilene, TX: Abilene Christian University Bookstore, 1980-1987; originally published 1920-1952).

6 Foy E. Wallace Jr., *The Christian and the Government* (Nashville, TN: Foy E. Wallace, Jr. Publications, 1968), 46.

7 Robert E. Hooper, *Crying in the Wilderness: A Biography of David Lipscomb* (Nashville, TN: David Lipscomb College, 1979) and Earl Irvin West, *The Life and Times of David Lipscomb* (Henderson, TN: Religious Book Service, 1954).

8 Don Carlos Janes, "J. A. Harding," *GH* 2 (14 May 1914), 1.

9 James A. Harding, "What are the Nashville Churches Doing?" *CLW* 24 (28 June 1910), 8.

10 Lloyd Cline Sears, *The Eyes of Jehovah: The Life and Faith of James Alexander*

Harding (Nashville, TN: Gospel Advocate Co., 1970).

11 Lloyd Cline Sears, *For Freedom: The Biography of John Nelson Armstrong* (Austin, TX: Sweet Publishing Co., 1969).

12 Thomas G. Bradshaw, *R. H. Boll: Controversy and Accomplishment Among Churches of Christ* (Louisville, KY: Word and Work Publishers, 1998).

13 See John Mark Hicks, "The Gracious Separatist: Moral and Positive Law in the Theology of James A. Harding," *RQ* 42.3 (2000), 129-144, available at http://johnmarkhicks.faithsite.com/content.asp?CID=17867.

14 Cf. Earl Irvin West, *Search for the Ancient Order* (Indianapolis: Religious Book Service, 1979), 3:270-3.

PART I: KINGDOM DYNAMICS

1 M. Norvel Young, *A History of Colleges Established and Controlled by Members of the Churches of Christ* (Kansas City: Old Paths Book Club, 1949), 75, 113, 118, and Sears, *For Freedom*, 75ff, 110ff.

2 Richard T. Hughes, *Reviving the Ancient Faith: The Story of Churches of Christ in America* (Grand Rapids: Eerdmans, 1996), 3: to live "life as if the final rule of the kingdom of God were present in the here and now."

3 R. C. Bell, "Honor to Whom Honor is Due," *FF* 68 (6 November 1951), 6.

CHAPTER TWO: SHADOWS OF THE SECOND COMING

1 Lipscomb, CG, 27 (emphasis in original).

2 Harding, "The Kingdom of Christ Vs. The Kingdoms of Satan," *The Way* 5 (15 October 1903), 930, available at http://www.mun.ca/rels/restmov/texts/jharding/KCVKS.HTM.

3 Harding, whose acquaintance with Lawrence goes back eighteen years to Detroit, describes Lawrence as "a good man, earnest and kind, gentle and true" ("Scraps," *The Way* 5 [15 October 1903], 929).

4 Harding, "The Kingdom of Christ," *The Way* 5 (15 October, 1903), 929-931. Cf. Lipscomb, "Christian to Leaven Human Government," *GA* 20 (8 August, 1878), 488.

5 Richard T. Hughes introduced the term "apocalyptic worldview" in "The Apocalyptic Origins of Churches of Christ and the Triumph of Modernism," *Religion and American Culture* 2 (Summer 1992), 181-214. The "apocalyptic worldview" is a posture that seeks fulfillment in this life as if the eschatological kingdom of God were fully present. We use the phrase "shadows of the second coming" to describe this powerful impulse in the NBST. Harding, according to Hughes, is the "epitome of the apocalyptic" vision of the NBST (*Reviving the Ancient Faith* [Grand Rapids: Eerdmans, 1996], 138).

6 Lipscomb, *CG*. Harding said, "Civil Government is the best book on the subject

of the Christian's duty to civil government in the world, so far as I know" ("Books," *The Way* 2 [May 1900], 71).

7 Harding, "The Kingdom of Christ," 930. Cf. Harding, "Man was Created to Reign For Ever and Ever," *CLW* 19 (6 June 1905), 8-9, available at http://www.mun.ca/rels/restmov/texts/jharding/MWCRFE.HTM

8 Lipscomb, *SS*, 114.

9 Boll, "The Kingdom of God," *WW* 10 (January 1916), 21-22.

10 Lipscomb, *CG*, 40.

11 Harding, "Kingdom of Christ, 931.

12 Lipscomb, *QA*, 247.

13 Lipscomb, "The Kingdom of God," *GA* 45 (21 May 1903), 328. This language appears in other places in Lipscomb. Writing twenty-five years earlier, he says, "the kingdom of God certainly embraces more than the church of God on earth. We have frequently written and spoken that the kingdom of God was coeval [sic] and co-extensive with the reign and authority of God." For Lipscomb the kingdom existed before Pentecost. It existed in an unorganized state in Israel, but since Pentecost the "churches are the development or manifestation of the kingdom" in the world. The church is where the values of the kingdom of God prevail. Cf. "The Kingdom of Heaven—When Set Up," *GA* 18 (4 May 1876), 420-424.

14 See John Howard Yoder, *The Politics of Jesus* (Grand Rapids: Eerdmans, 1972), 47. Being a "distinct" people is such an important motif in restoration thinking that Robert Hooper entitled his history *A Distinct People* (West Monroe, LA: Howard, 1993). David Edwin Harrell suggests that cultural separatism or a "sojourner" mentality describes the mindset of early twentieth-century Churches of Christ; *The Churches of Christ in the 20th Century: Homer Hailey's Personal Journey of Faith* (Tuscaloosa: UA Press, 2000), 71-73.

15 Cornelius Plantinga, Jr., *Not The Way It's Supposed to Be: A Breviary of Sin* (Grand Rapids: Eerdmans, 1995). Plantinga defines the essence of sin as the "vandalism" of God's *shalom*, esp. pp. 7-27.

16 Boll, "Kingdom of God," 22; cf. Boll, "What Shall the End Be?" *The Way* 2 (April 1900): 61-62.

17 Harding, "The Second Coming of Jesus - When Will it Be?" *The Way* 4 (25 September 1902), 203; reprinted "The Second Coming of Jesus—When will it Be?" *CLW* 23 (16 March 1909), 8-9.

18 Lipscomb, *CG*, 96.

19 Richard Hughes, *Reclaiming A Heritage* (Abilene: ACU Press, 2002), 8. Cf. pgs 68-69, 75.

20 See David A. DeSilva, *Perseverance in Gratitude: A Socio-Rhetorical Commentary on the Epistle 'to the Hebrews'* (Grand Rapids: Eerdmans, 2000), 392-405, esp. 394-395.

21 Justin Martyr, *First Apology*, 14, available at http://www.newadvent.org/fathers/0126.htm.

22 Stanley Hauerwas and William H. Willimon, *Resident Aliens* (Nashville: Abingdon, 1989), 46.

23 Harding, "To Whom Was The Sermon on the Mount Addressed? A Reply to Doctor Holloway," *CLW* 20 (3 April 1906), 8-9, and "Saving Souls, Special Providence, Dr. Holloway," *CLW* 21 (29 January 1907), 8.

24 Lipscomb, *CG*, 133

25 The two cities in Revelation function rhetorically to call Christians to a counter-cultural life; cf. Barbara R. Rossing, *The Choice Between Two Cities: Whore, Bride, and Empire in the Apocalypse* (Harrisburg, PA: Trinity Press, 1999).

26 Roland H. Bainton, *Christian Attitudes Toward War and Peace* (Nashville: Abingdon, 1960): 66-84

27 *The Epistle to Diognetus*, 5 in J. B. Lightfoot, *The Apostolic Fathers* (Grand Rapids: Baker Reprint, 1986), 253-254.

28 Lipscomb, *CG*, 133.

29 Mark A. Noll, *Turning Points: Decisive Moments in the History of Christianity* (Grand Rapids: Baker, 1997), 88.

30 Robert E. Hooper, *Crying in the Wilderness: A Biography of David Lipscomb* (Nashville: David Lipscomb College, 1979), 98. Lipscomb appeals to the example of the Anabaptists in *CG*, 123-126.

31 Lipscomb, *CG*, 128.

32 Yoder, *Politics of Jesus*, 226-227.

33 Lee Camp, *Mere Discipleship: Radical Christianity in a Rebellious World* (Grand Rapids: Brazos Press, 2003), 137-149.

CHAPTER THREE: GOD STILL WORKS

1 Harding, "Scraps," *The Way* 3 (27 February 1902), 370.

2 Lipscomb, "Providence—Special and General," *GA* 10 (21 January 1869), 49-50.

3 September 23, 1863 to June 26, 1864.

4 T. B. Larimore, "David Lipscomb," *Christian Standard* 54 (22 December 1917), 391.

5 These opening paragraphs draw upon Hooper, *Crying in the Wilderness*, 82-86.

6 Hooper, *Crying in the Wilderness*, 146.

7 Mary Noxie Harding (March 21, 1874 to July 9, 1874) and Captain Jinks Harding (July 15, 1875 to June 1876).

8 Jess Cobb Harding (September 17, 1884 to July 10, 1891), Paul Travers Harding (October 29, 1891 to July 13, 1913), and David Allen Harding (July 16,

1893 to August 10, 1906).

9 Lloyd Cline Sears, *The Eyes of Jehovah: The Life and Faith of James Alexander Harding* (Nashville: Gospel Advocate, 1970), 18-23, 143, 213-214, 256.

10 Lipscomb, "God Uses the Evil as Well as the Good," *GA* 22 (30 September 1880), 634.

11 Ibid.

12 Sears, *The Eyes of Jehovah*, 32.

13 Harding, "Does God Work Miracles Now?" *GA* 26 (5 March 1884), 154.

14 Hiram Christopher, *The Relations of God to the World by 1. Immanency. 2. Intervention. 3. Incarnation* (Nashville: Gospel Advocate, 1900). Cf. John Mark Hicks, "Theodicy in Early Stone-Campbell Perspectives," in *Restoring the First Century Church in the Twenty-first Century: Essays on the Stone-Campbell Restoration Movement, In Honor of Don Haymes*, eds. Warren Lewis and Hans Rollmann (Eugene, OR: Wipf and Stock, 2005), 287-310.

15 George T. Smith, "Is There a Special Providence?" *Christian Standard* 15 (28 February 1880), 65 and S. H. Brown, "Sickness and Death Governed by Law, not Providence," *Christian Standard* 49 (31 May 1913), 890. See the discussion between Joseph Lowe and R. P. Anderson's responses in *Christian Standard* 31 (21 September 1895), 902, (12 October 1895), 975, and (16 November 1895), 1094.

16 Isaac Errett, "Prayer and Providence," *Christian Standard* 15 (17 January 1880), 20; (24 January 1880), 28.

17 Also Joseph H. Fox, *Special and General Providence* (St. Louis: John Burns, 1880) and J. S. Lamar, "What Most Interests Me Now," *Christian-Evangelist* 38 (28 March 28 1901), 393-4.

18 Lipscomb, "Providence," 50.

19 Harding, "Evangelist," 8.

20 Harding, "The Evangelist, His Support, Etc.," *CLW* 18 (9 August 1904), 8.

21 Harding, "Man Was Created to Reign for Ever and Ever," *CLW* 19 (6 June 1905), 8.

22 *SS*, 403-4.

23 *QA*, 257.

24 Lipscomb, "God," 42.

25 Harding, "How Does God Help His People?" *CLW* 20 (6 February 6 1906), 8.

26 Harding and White, *The Harding-White Discussion* (Cincinnati: Rowe, 1910), available at http://www.mun.ca/rels/restmov/texts/jharding/hw.htm.

27 Ibid.

28 Harding, "The Invisible Miracles of the Bible," *CLW* 18 (6 September 1904), 8.

29 Harding, "Thought on Miracles," *GA* 26 (27 February 1884), 131.

30 Ibid.

31 Harding, "Angels and Miracles," *CLW* 20 (8 May 8 1906), 8; "Does God Work Miracles Now?" *GA* 26 (5 March 1884), 154; "Prayers for the Sick," *The Way* 3 (9 May 1901), 41-43; "The Invisible Miracles of the Bible," *CLW* 18 (6 September 1904), 8-9.

32 Harding, "Prayer for the Sick," *The Way* 3 (9 May 1901), 42.

33 Harding, "Prayer for the Sick," 41.

34 Harding, "Scraps," *GA* 29 (20 April 1887), 252.

35 Harding, "Scraps," *The Way* 4 (19 June 1902), 90.

36 Harding, "Temporal Blessings," *GA* 25 (5 September 1883), 570; "Temporal Blessings—No. 2," *GA* 25 (12 September 1883), 586; and "Temporal Blessings—No. 3," *GA* 25 (19 September 1883), 602.

37 Harding, "The Contract Which God Proposes to His Children," *CLW* 20 (20 November 1906), 8-9.

38 Harding, "Three Contradictory Theories," *The Way* 3 (4 April 1901), 4.

39 Harding, "Scraps," *The Way* 4.2 (10 April 1902), 10.

40 Harding, "A Statement for My Critics" *GA* 26 (13 February 1884), 106. "I am certain that my motives in writing this will be misconstrued, and that mercenary considerations will be attributed to me; but that in no wise moves me; if some young man by reading this has his heart stirred as mine was upon reading the biography of Samuel Rogers; if his attention is fixed by it upon the precious promises of our Lord, so that he may be induced to give himself wholly, body, soul and spirit, to the grand work, I will have accomplished enough to counterbalance all such evil surmisings." Cf. Samuel Rogers, *Autobiography of Elder Samuel Rogers*, ed. John Rogers, 4th ed (Cincinnati: Standard Publishing, 1909), 11-12.

41 Harding, "Scraps. For God Was With Him," *CLW* 18 (2 February 1904), 8-9.

42 Lyrics from http://library.timelesstruths.org/music/Living_by_Faith/.

CHAPTER FOUR: HOLY SPIRIT

1 Harding, "Questions and Answers," *The Way* 4 (17 July 1902), 123.

2 Harding, "Notes on the Holy Spirit's Work, with a Remarkable Illustration," *CLW* (1 August 1905), 8.

3 Harding, "How Does God Help His People?" *CLW* 20 (6 February 1906), 8-9.

4 Paul K. Conkin, *Cane Ridge: America's Pentecost* (Madison: University of Wisconsin, 1990).

5 Walter Scott, *A Discourse on the Holy Spirit* (Bethany, VA: Alexander Campbell, 1831), available at http://www.mun.ca/rels/restmov/texts/acampbell/tmh/MH0214.HTM

6 Robert Richardson, "Simplification, No. 2," *The Evangelist* 3 (3 March 1834),

52. Richardson is perceptive enough to see what many word only advocates did not. Biblical phrases like "word of God" and "the Word" do not refer to a written page. Rather they refer to an oral message (as in the prophets), the gospel message, or to the person of Christ himself.

7 Harding, "Indwelling of Demons and of the Holy Spirit," *CLW* 22 (12 May 1908), 8.

8 Timothy Weber, *Living in the Shadow of the Second Coming: American Premillennialism, 1875-1982* (Grand Rapids: Zondervan, 1983), 40.

9 Stanford Chambers, "It is to Reminisce," *The Exhorter* 1 (1 January 1968), 4.

10 Armstrong, "Words of Commendation," *GA* 45 (22 November 1903), 461; Boll, "James A. Harding," *WW* 15 (May 1922), 164; R. C. Bell, "Honor to Whom Honor is Due," *FF* 68 (6 November 1951), 6.

11 R. L. Whiteside, "Indwelling of the Holy Spirit," *GH* 1 (28 August 1913), 2: "Recently some writers have sought to make the impression that the doctrine of the indwelling of the Holy Spirit is a new doctrine taught principally by the Bible schools." Though a student of Harding's at the NBS, he disagreed with Harding at almost every point in relation to the NBST. He became, we believe, one of the major theological architects for the "TT."

12 Biographical information on Holloway is scant. His picture is included in D. S. Ligon's *Portraiture of Gospel Preachers* in 1899. He had articles in the *Christian Record*, *Christian Leader and the Way*, *Gospel Guide* and edited the *Defender of the Word.* He died in 1912 in Chicago after ministering in Illinois. "Death of Dr. J.C. Holloway," *Christian Leader* 26 (9 September 1912), 13.

13 Holloway, "Another Article by Dr. J.C. Holloway," *CLW* 20 (13 February 1906), 5.

14 From 1905 to 1906 the *CLW* published 76 pieces on the Holy Spirit, ranging from short letters to several page articles. Of these, 19 come from the pen of Holloway and 11 from Harding.

15 J. S. Warlick, *Gospel Guide* 1 (1 June 1905), 63. Concerning Holloway's position, Warlick writes, "I am glad to find him right on the [Spirit] question."

16 Holloway, "Personal Indwelling of the Holy Spirit - 1," *CLW* 19 (9 May 1905), 1. Cf. also "Regeneration and Renewing of the Holy Spirit," *CLW* 19 (21 March 1905), 5.

17 Human ability is a significant theme for Holloway. Even the fruit of the Spirit is the result of human effort. "I have already told you that he that heareth [sic] the Word of God…can bear fruit even an hundred fold!" "A Word to Bro. Boll," *CLW* 19 (23 May 1905), 4.

18 Holloway, "Personal Indwelling of the Holy Spirit - 2," *CLW* 19 (16 May 1905), 9.

19 Holloway, "Personal Indwelling of the Holy Spirit -3," *CLW* 19 (23 May 1905), 4; Emphasis in original.

20 Holloway, *The Spirit and the Word* (Evansville, IND: Keller Printing & Publishing, 1905), 23, 26-27.

21 Holloway, *The Spirit and the Word*, 51 (emphasis in original).

22 Harding, "What Does the Promise 'Lo, I am with You Always' Mean to the Modern Evangelist," *CLW* 18 (16 August 1904), 8.

23 Harding, "How Does God Help His People?" *CLW* 20 (6 February 1906), 8. Cf. "What Help Do We Receive from God in Answer to Prayer?" *CLW* 19 (14 February 1905), 8-9; "Prayer for the Sick," *The Way* 3 (9 May 1901), 41-43.

24 Harding, "The Greatest Hindrance to the Spread of the Gospel," *The Way* 3 (6 March 1902), 378. Lipscomb and Harding were not of one mind on this point. Lipscomb was much more likely to speak of the world as subjected to law and order by divine arrangement, cf. *SS*, 9, 76-79, 84-85. Lipscomb, however, did believe in divine intervention.

25 Harding, "What I Would Not, I Do," *GA* 25 (11 July 1883), 442.

26 Harding, "Notes on the Holy Spirit's Work," 8.

27 Harding, "From Exchanges, " *The Way* 2 (April 1900), 50. Cf. also "Three Lessons From the Book of Romans," in *Biographies and Sermons*, ed. F. D. Srygley (Nashville: McQuiddy Publishing, 1898), 242-252, available at http://www.mun.ca/rels/restmov/texts/jharding/TLFBR.HTM

28 Harding, "The Gift of the Holy Spirit," *The Way* 2 (August 1900), 115-116: "The Holy Spirit—A Bible Reading," *The Way* 1 (1 August 1899), 114-118. This article was reprinted numerous times and represents a fairly complete summary of his doctrine of the Holy Spirit. Cf. *CLW* 18 (31 May 1904), 8-9; *CLW* 18 (7 June 1904), 8-9; and *GH* 1 (29 May 1913), 1; available at http://www.mun.ca/rels/restmov/ texts/jharding/HSABR.HTM

29 Harding, "Atlanta—God's Providence—The Holy Spirit," *CLW* 20 (19 June 1906), 9.

30 Harding, "Another Effort to Get Dr. Holloway Out of the Fog," *CLW* 19 (24 October 1905), 8.

31 Harding, "The Holy Spirit: Does He Dwell in Us? What Does He Do for Us?" *CLW* 19 (13 June 1905), 9.

32 Harding, "How Does God Help His People?" 8.

33 Boll, "The Spirit's Indwelling," *CLW* 19 (16 May 1905), 1.

34 Harding, "The Holy Spirit: A Reply to Dr. Holloway, Pt. 1 & Pt. 2," *CLW* 19 (22 August 1905), 8.

35 Harding, "The Holy Spirit: A Reply to Dr. Holloway," 8-9; "The Gift of the Holy Spirit: A Reply to Dr. Holloway," *CLW* 19 (25 July 1905), 8-9.

36 Harding, "The Holy Spirit in the Church," *CLW* 19 (28 February 1905), 8.

37 Harding, "The Holy Spirit: Does He Dwell in Us?" 8.

38 Ibid.

39 Holloway, quoted in James A. Harding, "Saving Souls, Special Providence, Dr. Holloway," *CLW* 21 (29 January 1904), 8.

40 Holloway, "Brother Harding's Foggy Effort," *CLW* 19 (21 November 1905), 3.

41 Harding, "Saving Souls, Special Providence, Dr. Holloway," 8.

42 Wilf Hildebrandt, *An Old Testament Theology of the Spirit of God* (Peabody, MA: Hendrickson, 1995), 67-72.

43 See Roger Stronstad, *The Charismatic Theology of St. Luke* (Peabody, MA: Hendrickson, 1984).

44 Gordon D. Fee, *God's Empowering Presence: The Holy Spirit in the Letters of Paul* (Peabody, MA: Hendrickson, 1994), 872.

45 Joachim Jeremias, *The Central Message of the New Testament* (Philadelphia: Fortress Press, 1965), 9-30; cf. Michael Green, *I Believe in the Holy Spirit* (Grand Rapids: Eerdmans, Revised, 2004), 63.

46 Harding, "The Holy Spirit— A Bible Reading," 118; "The Gift of the Holy Spirit," *The Way* 2 (August 1900), 118.

47 Harding, "Brother Crownover's Question Concerning the Holy Spirit," *CLW* 19 (4 April 1905), 8.

48 Harding often speaks of being miraculously "led" by God; "Thoughts on Miracles," *GA* 26 (27 February 1884), 131.

49 R. L. Whiteside, *Annual Lesson Commentary on Bible School Lessons,* 1940 (Nashville: Gospel Advocate, 1939), 182-187.

50 C. R. Nichol and R. L. Whiteside, *Sound Doctrine* (Clifton, TX: Nichol Publishing, 1924), 4:107-108.

51 R. L. Whiteside, "The Word of God," *Gospel Guide* 2 (1 May 1906), 42-43; "Doctrinal Discourses: The Uses of Scripture," *GA* 74 (4 February 1932), 138; "The Word of God and Our Attitude Toward It," *GH* 1 (21 November 1912), 1; "The Seed of the Kingdom," *GH* 1 (28 November 1912), 1.

52 R. L. Whiteside, "The Gospel of Christ," *GA* 44 (20 February 1902), 125.

53 H. Leo Boles, *The Holy Spirit, His Personality, Nature, Works* (Nashville: Gospel Advocate, 1942), 204, 207, 241.

54 Use the *Lectio Divina* methodology discussed in chapter 4. Bernard of Clairvaux may be a good companion in reading the Song of Songs this way. He may help with simply enjoying God. Cf. *Bernard of Clairvaux: Classics of Western Spirituality*, ed. G. R. Evans (Paulist Press, 1987).

PART II: KINGDOM SPIRITUALITY

1 Harding, "Scraps," *GA* 27 (9 February 1887), 88.

2 F. W. Emmons of Emmaus, Indiana (cf. Alexander Campbell, "Order of Worship," *MH* 2ns [June 1838], 247-250) and Alfred Elmore of Covington, Indiana (cf. "Salutatory" *GA* 43 [21 March 1901], 186). Several ministers in Texas at the beginning of the 20th century also supported this view through the *Gospel Missionary*; cf. Stephen Daniel Eckstein, *History of the Churches of Christ in Texas, 1824-1950* (Austin, TX: Firm Foundation Publishing House, 1963), 265-266.

3 Harding, "The Habits that Save," *The Way* 4 (5 February 1903), 356

4 Harding, "Questions Concerning the Way to Heaven," *The Way* 4 (12 February 1903), 370.

5 Harding, "Questions and Answers," *The Way* 4 (17 July 1902), 123.

6 Harding, "Scraps," *The Way* 5 (23 July 1903), 735.

7 Harding, "Scraps," *The Way* 5 (15 October 1903), 945.

8 Harding, "About Protracted Meetings," *GA* 27 (14 September 1887), 588.

9 Harding, "Ira C. Moore on the Validity of Baptism," *CLW* 23 (18 May 1909), 8.

10 Harding, "Scraps," *The Way* 4 (26 February 1903), 401-2.

CHAPTER FIVE: LISTENING TO GOD

1 Harding, "The Great Increase of Bible Study in America," *CLW* 22 (10 November 1908), 8

2 Boll, *Lessons on Hebrews* (Nashville, TN: McQuiddy Printing Company, 1910), 4-5, available at http://www.mun.ca/rels/restmov/texts/rboll/loh1/LOH100E.HTM.

3 Walter Scott Priest, "Bible-Trained Men in Places of Power," in *Centennial Convention Report*, ed. W. R. Warren (Cincinnati: Christian Standard Publishing, 1910), 557.

4 Campbell, "Bible Reading," *MH* 3ns (January 1839), 36, available at http://www.mun.ca/rels/restmov/texts/acampbell/mh1839/BIBREAD.HTM.

5 Harding, "Does God Work Miracles Now?" *GA* 26 (5 March 1884), 154.

6 Priest, "Bible-Trained," 558.

7 Boll, "James A. Harding," *WW* 15 (June 1922), 164, available at http://www.mun.ca/rels/restmov/texts/rboll/jaharding.html.

8 Harding, "The Bible," *GA* 25 (16 October 1883), 666.

9 Harding, "The Two Bible Readings," *GA* 28 (27 January 1886), 51.

10 Harding, *Debate on Baptism and the Work of the Holy Spirit* (Nashville: Gospel Advocate, 1955 reprint), 38.

11 Harding, "What Way? How Do You Get Into It? How Do You Travel It?" *The Way* 1 (26 January 1899), 2.

12 Harding, "Scraps," *GA* 29 (23 February 1887), 120.

13 Ibid.

14 Harding, "Miracles," 154.

15 Harding, "The Whiskey Traffic and an Inefficient Eldership," *CLW* 22 (15 December 1908), 8-9.

16 Harding, "The Preacher and His Pay," *GA* 30 (18 January 1888), 3

17 Harding, "Scraps," *The Way* 3 (19 September 1901), 193.

18 Harding, "Two Bible Readings," 51.

19 Harding, "The Higher Criticism: Some Wonderful Things About It," *The Way* 5 (23 April 1903), 530.

20 Don Carlos Janes, "J. A. Harding," *GH* 2 (14 May 1914), 1

21 Harding, "Miracles," 154.

22 Harding, "Regular Reading vs. Topical Study," *GA* 29 (3 August 1887), 481

23 Harding, "Two Bible Readings," 51.

24 Justin Martyr, *First Apology*, 67, available at http://www.newadvent.org/fathers/0126.htm.

25 Campbell, *Christian System* (Nashville, TN: Gospel Advocate, 1970 reprint), 3.

26 Robert Richardson, *Memoirs of Alexander Campbell* (Philadelphia: J.P. Lippincott & Co., 1868), I:143, available at http://www.mun.ca/rels/restmov/texts/rrichardson/mac/MAC109.HTM#Page142

27 Campbell, "On Bible Reading—No. I," *MH* 3ns (August 1839), 344, available at http://www.mun.ca/rels/restmov/texts/acampbell/mh1839/SSCP4.HTM.

28 Campbell, "Bible Reading" *MH* 3ns (January 1839), 37.

29 Kenneth Cukrowski, Mark W. Hamilton and James W. Thompson, *God's Holy Fire: The Nature and Function of Scripture* (Abilene: ACU Press, 2002), 6-10.

30 Several websites assist readers with a daily Bible program that will enable this kind of story-formed reading of Scripture. See http://www.backtothebible.org/devotions/journey/ or http://www.thebible.net/read/sched.html. Also, the "One Year Bible" is a helpful tool, as well as F. LaGard Smith, ed., *Narrated Bible in Chronological Order* (Eugene, OR: Harvest House Publishers, 1999).

31 Campbell, "Bible Reading" *MH* 3ns (January 1839), 37.

32 We recommend the series of meditative guides authored by Gary Holloway and Earl Lavendar through Leafwood Press. Cf. Gary Holloway, *Matthew: Jesus is King* (Siloam Springs, AR: Leafwood Press, 2005).

33 Harding, "How to Fall in Love with the Bible," *GH* 3 (20 May 1915), 1.

34 One of the formative pieces for this analogy is N.T. Wright, "How Can the Bible be Authoritative?," *Vox Evangelica* 21 (1991), 7-32, available at http://

www.ntwrightpage.com/Wright_Bible_Authoritative.htm.

35 Harding, "Great Increase," 8.

CHAPTER SIX: RELEASING THE OPPRESSED

1 Lipscomb, "Fellowship," *GA* 9 (13 June 1867), 476.

2 Lipscomb, "Who Are to Blame?" *GA* 11 (6 May 1869), 422. Lipscomb uses the startling phrase "God's elect" in reference to the poor on numerous occasions. Cf, "Preaching to the Poor," *GA* 15 (28 May 1873), 511; "New Publications," *GA* 8 (1 January 1866), 12. Cf. Anthony L. Dunnavant "David Lipscomb and the 'Preferential Option for the Poor' among Postbellum Churches of Christ" in *The Stone-Campbell Movement: An International Religious Tradition*, eds., Michael W. Casey and Douglas A. Foster (Knoxville: UT Press, 2002), 435-454.

3 R. H. Boll, "The Kingdom of the Lowly," *The Way* 1 (1 August 1899), 126.

4 See Eric Foner and Olivia Mahoney, *America's Reconstruction: People and Politics After the Civil War* (New York: HaperPerennial, 1995).

5 Jacqueline Jones, *The Dispossessed: America's Underclass from the Civil War to the Present* (New York: Basic Books, 1992), 13-70.

6 The Populist Party emerged in the 1880s among farmers and industrial workers who shared grievances against big business practices. See "The Populist Party" available at http://projects.vassar.edu/1896/populists.html

7 Samuel Gompers, quoted in Harvie M. Conn, *The American City and the Evangelical Church: A Historical Overview* (Grand Rapids: Baker, 1994), 66.

8 Quoted in David Edwin Harrell, Jr., "The Agrarian Myth and the Disciples of Christ in the Nineteenth Century," *Agricultural History* 41 (April 1967), 189.

9 Lipscomb, "Preaching to the Poor," *GA* 15 (24 April 1873), 390.

10 Ibid., 391.

11 Lipscomb, "Preaching to the Poor," *GA* 15 (28 May 1873), 512.

12 Robert E. Hooper, *Crying in the Wilderness: A Biography of David Lipscomb* (Nashville: David Lipscomb College, 1979), 222-234; Anthony Dunnavant, "David Lipscomb on the Church and the Poor," *RQ* 33 (1991): 75-85.

13 David Edwin Harrell, Jr. characterizes this effort as "spectacular," *The Social Sources of Division in the Disciples of Christ, 1865-1900: A Social History of the Disciples of Christ, Vol. 2* (Atlanta and Athens: Publishing Systems, Inc., 1973), 54. On the hundred thousand dollar figure see David Lipscomb, "Thirty Years' Work," *GA* 38 (2 January 1896), 4.

14 Lipscomb, "The Destitution South," *GA* 9 (28 February 1867), 171.

15 Lipscomb, "A Word to Our Southern Brethren," *GA* 8 (27 November 1866), 758.

16 Letter to Fanning and Lipscomb, *GA* 8 (6 February 1866), 88.

17 Lipscomb, "Fellowship," *GA* 8 (22 May 1866), 335-336; see "Fellowship" *GA* 8 (25 September 1866), 623 and "Dispensing Christian Fellowship," *GA* 8 (24 July 1866), 473-474.

18 Lipscomb, "A Word to Our Southern Brethren," 758.

19 Lipscomb, "Fellowship," *GA* 9 (13 June 1867), 476.

20 Lipscomb, "The Cholera," *GA* 15 (26 June 1873), 619.

21 Lipscomb, "The Cholera and the Christian Religion," *GA* 15 (17 July 1873), 649-653.

22 Hooper, *Crying in the Wilderness*, 136.

23 Lipscomb, "Aid to Christians in Need – How Shall It Be Administered?" *GA* 12 (17 March 1870), 253.

24 Lipscomb, "Dispensing Christian Fellowship," *GA* 8 (24 July 1866), 473-474.

25 Lipscomb, "The Cholera and The Christian Religion," 649.

26 Lipscomb, "Destitution South," 171-172.

27 Hooper, *Crying in the Wilderness*, 22-23.

28 Cf. the report by Hans Rollmann at http://bible.acu.edu/sc/Default.asp?Bookmark=45940

29 Lipscomb, "Some Thoughts Suggested by the Political Contest," *GA* 38 (12 November 1896), 724.

30 Lipscomb, "Race Prejudice," *GA* 20 (21 February 1878), 120.

31 Ibid., 121.

32 Lipscomb, "The Negro in the Worship—A Correspondence," *GA* 44 (4 July 1907), 425; available at http://www.mun.ca/rels/restmov/texts/race/negro.html

33 John H. Cain, "Religion and Politics," *GA* 22 (9 September 1880), 575.

34 Lipscomb, "Christ the Savior of the World," *GA* 8 (20 February 1866), 124.

35 Lipscomb, "Shall Christians Administer to the Aliens?" *GA* 10 (29 October 1868), 1048-1049.

36 The Exodus is a powerful symbol of redemption for people through the centuries. Of interest is the different ways white Christians have read the story and they way black slaves in America interpreted it. A sensitive telling of these two contrasting interpretations can be found in David W. Kling, *The Bible in History: How the Texts Have Shaped the Times* (New York: Oxford University Press, 2004), 193-229.

37 James A. Sanders and Craig Evans, *Luke and Scripture: The Function of Sacred Tradition in Luke-Acts* (Augsburg/Fortress, 1993), 84-94; John Howard Yoder, *The Politics of Jesus* (Grand Rapids: Eerdmans, 1972), 64-77. For an insightful treatment of the ethical value of the year of Jubilee in the Old Testament see Christopher J. H. Wright, *Walking in the Ways of the Lord: The Ethical Authority of the Old Testament* (Downers Grove, IVP, 1996).

38 Ronald J. Sider, *Good News and Good Works: A Theology for the Whole Gospel*

(Grand Rapids: Baker, 1999), 89.

39 David Lipscomb, *SS*, 114.

40 Lipscomb, "Who Are to Blame?" *GA* 11 (6 May 1869), 425; cf. "Christ and the Working People," *GA* 38 (4 June 1896), 356.

41 Lipscomb, "Objects to be Accomplished by a Church," *GA* 10 (19 November 1868), 2009.

42 W. A. Cameron, *The ORIGIN and DEVELOPMENT of the NEGRO RACE*, (St. Petersburg: Westbrook Printing, 1954).

43 Ibid., 7.

44 Richard Hughes, *Reviving the Ancient Faith* (Grand Rapids: Eerdmans, 1996), 204.

45 Harold Shank, "Nashville's Central Church of Christ: The First Twenty Years," *RQ* 41 (1999), 12. Cf. "Real Religion—The Ministry of E. H. Ijams," *RQ* 47 (2005): 221-236.

46 Quoted in Hughes, *Reviving the Ancient Faith*, 205.

47 A. M. Burton, "We Did Not Have to Think It Out; It Was Found in the Bible. Read Matt. 25:34-36," *LM* 4 (1 July 1926), 405.

48 Shank, "Nashville's Central Church," 15-16.

49 Burton, "We Did Not Have to Think It Out," 406.

CHAPTER SEVEN: COMMUNING WITH GOD

1 Boll, *The Kingdom of God*, 3rd ed., revised (Louisville, KY: Word and Work, 2000), 46, available at http://www.mun.ca/rels/restmov/texts/rboll/kog3r/KOG3R07.HTM.

2 Lipscomb, "The Lord's Day Meeting," *GA* 13 (15 June 1871), 558.

3 G. G. Taylor, *A History of the Plum Street Church of Christ, Detroit, Mich.* (Cincinnati, Ohio: F. L. Rowe, Publishers, 1906), 56-57.

4 Harding, "The Plum Street Church of Detroit, Michigan," *GA* 24 (11 May 1882), 298-99.

5 Taylor, *History*, 16-48.

6 Ibid., 50.

7 Harding, "The Church of Christ, Plum St., Detroit, Mich.," *The Old Path Guide* 3 (May 1881), 266-8. See also "The Plum Street Church," *GA* 27 (25 November 1885), 748 and "Scraps," *GA* 29 (9 February 1887), 88.

8 Alexander Campbell, *Christian Baptism with its Antecedents and Consequents* (Bethany: Campbell, 1851), 246-247, available at http://www.mun.ca/rels/restmov/texts/acampbell/cbac/CBAC401.HTM.

9 Richardson, *Memoirs*, 2:223, available at http://www.mun.ca/rels/restmov/texts/rrichardson/mac/MAC206.HTM.

10 Alexander Campbell, "Dialogue on Heresy," *MH* 3 (August 1832), 404, available at http://www.mun.ca/rels/restmov/texts/acampbell/tmh/MH0308.HTM.

11 Campbell, "Fact," *MH Extra* 4 (August 1833), 341.

12 Q&A, 319.

13 *Q&A*, 174.

14 Ibid.

15 Harding, "Scraps," *The Way* 4 (17 April 1902), 17.

16 *Q&A*, 267.

17 Lipscomb, "The Flesh and Blood—The Lord's Supper," *GA* 10 (23 April 1868), 391.

18 Harding, "The Church of God at Valdosta, GA," *GA* 25 (15 February 1883), 102

19 Lipscomb, "The Flesh and Blood," 391.

20 *Q&A*, 266.

21 *Q&A*, 267.

22 Harding, "An Interesting Letter from C. E. J.," *The Way* 5 (9 July 1903), 707.

23 Harding, "The Pastor—A Letter from Brother J. E. Dunn and a Reply by the Editor," *The Way* 2 (June 1900), 84.

24 Harding, "An Interesting Letter," 707.

25 Lipscomb, "Lord's Day Meeting," 557.

26 Lipscomb, "Lord's Day Meeting," 557.

27 Geron Davis, "Holy Ground," lyrics available at http://www.audible-faith.com/pages/sg200104.

28 See John Mark's blogs concerning Sheila and Joshua at http://professing-professor.blogspot.com/2005/05/four-years-ago-today.html and http://profess-ingprofessor.blogspot.com/2005/05/remembering-yesterday-but-enjoying.html.

CHAPTER EIGHT: CRYING FOR THE KINGDOM

1 Harding, "Questions and Answers," *The Way* 4 (17 July 1902), 123.

2 Harding, "Does God Answer Prayer?" *CLW* 19 (19 September 1905), 8.

3 James A. Harding and L. S. White, *The Harding -White Discussion* (Cincinnati: F. L. Rowe, 1910), 18. Available at http://www.mun.ca/rels/restmov/texts/jhard-ing/hw.htm

4 Ibid., 19.

5 Harding, *Harding-White Discussion*, 25.

6 Harding, "Give Us this Day our Daily Bread," *CLW* 23 (30 March 1909), 8. Campbell had overthrown sectarianism.

7 Harding told White he had been "well informed" concerning Mueller for "twenty years" which would be around 1890, *Harding-White Discussion*, 25. Through

his journals Harding promoted Mueller as an example to follow and encouraged readers to buy his biography offered through *The Way*, cf. "George Mueller," *The Way* 1 (25 February 1899), 32; "A Busy Man and His Bible," *The Way* 2 (May 1900), 79. See *George Muller of Bristol and His Witness to a Prayer-Hearing God* by Arthur T. Pierson (Old Tappen, NJ: Fleming H. Revell, 1899), available at http://www.bible-believers.com/george_muller/ Muller has remained sort of an icon of the premillennial Churches of Christ.

8 Harding, *Harding-White Discussion*, 25.

9 Harding, "Scraps," *The Way* 3 (5 December 1901), 282.

10 Stanley J. Grenz has argued persuasively that Christian prayer is nothing less than God's people pleading for the full establishment of the kingdom of God, *Prayer: The Cry for the Kingdom*, Revised (Grand Rapids: Eerdmans, 2005).

11 Harding, "Pray Ye To The Lord Of The Harvest," *GA* 25 (18 January 1883), 38.

12 Harding, *Harding-White Discussion*, 3.

13 Harding, "Scraps," *The Way* 3 (5 December 1901), 282.

14 Harding, "Praying for Rain," *The Way* 3 (28 November 1901), 276.

15 Harding, "Prayer for the Sick," *The Way* 3 (9 May 1901), 41.

16 Harding, "Scraps," *GA* 29 (9 February 1887), 88.

17 Harding, "About Protracted Meetings," *GA* 29 (14 September 1887), 588.

18 This is a pervasive theme in Harding, cf. "The Most Perfect of All Societies," *CLW* 18 (2 August 1904), 9; "The Greatest Hindrance to the Spread of the Gospel," *The Way* 3 (6 March 1903), 378-379; "If it is so, Account for these Facts," *The Way* 3 (23 January 1902), 330-332; "Scraps," *The Way* 4 (10 April 1902), 9-12; "What Is It To Trust God - Who Does It?" *The Way* 4 (31 July 1902), 137-140; "Questions about Special Providence," *The Way* 4 (16 April 1903), 514-516; "Why This Unbelief?" *GH* 1 (8 May 1913), 3, 6.

19 Harding, "What Help Do We Receive From God in Answer to Prayer?" *CLW* 19 (14 February 1905), 8.

20 Harding, "How Does God Help His People?" *CLW* 20 (6 February 1906), 8.

21 Harding, "Praying for Rain," 276.

22 Harding, "What Way? How do you get into it? How do you travel it?" *The Way* 1 (26 January 1899), 2.

23 Harding, "The Whiskey Traffic and an Inefficient Eldership," *CLW* 22 (15 December 1908), 8-9.

24 Harding, "The Whiskey Traffic and an Inefficient Eldership," *CLW* 22 (15 December 1908), 8-9;

25 Harding, "Scraps," *CLW* 3 (5 December 1901), 282.

26 Harding, "The Web and Weft of Prayer," *The Way* 5 (19 November 1903),

1020-1021.

27 R. H. Boll, "The Reign of Money," *LM* 2 (14 August 1924), 332.

28 Eugene H. Peterson, *Answering God: The Psalms As Tools for Prayer* (San Francisco: HarperSanFrancisco, 1991), 59-67.

29 Greg Sterling, "'Pray Always':" Prayer in Luke/Acts" in *Preaching from Luke/Acts*, eds. David Fleer and David Bland (Abilene, TX: ACU Press, 2000), 67-88.

30 Eugene H. Peterson, *Christ Plays in Ten Thousand Places: A Conversation in Spiritual Theology* (Grand Rapids: Eerdmans, 2005), 273-276. These five prayers are Luke 1.38; 1:46-55; 1:68-79; 2.14; 2.29-32.

31 Ibid., 273.

32 Ibid., 276.

33 Ibid., 281.

34 Cf. D. A. Carson, *A Call to Spiritual Reformation: Priorities from Paul and His Prayers* (Grand Rapids: Baker, 1992)..

35 Grenz, *Prayer*, 53.

36 Cf. Gary Holloway and Earl Lavender, *Living God's Love: An Invitation to Christian Spirituality* (Siloam Springs, AR: Leafwood, 2004), 18.

37 "Anthem: Do Not Remember," in *The Prymer*, translated and adapted by Robert E. Webber (Brewster, MA: Paraclete Press, 2000), 96.

38 Moses quotes Exodus 34:6-7 back to Yahweh in his prayer.

PART III: KINGDOM LIFE

1 Robert H. Boll, *Paul's Letter to the Galatians* (Louisville, KY: Word and Work, 1951), 28, available at http://www.mun.ca/rels/restmov/texts/rboll/plg/PLG10.HTM.

CHAPTER NINE: THE PRINCE OF PEACE

1 Campbell, "An Address on War," available at http://www.mun.ca/rels/restmov/texts/acampbell/ac2.html

2 Lipscomb, *CG*, 10.

3 A copy of the petition is preserved by Lipscomb, *CG*, 128-130.

4 A copy of the petition given to Union official is preserved by Lipscomb, *CG*, 130-132.

5 Quoted in Robert E. Hooper, *Crying in the Wilderness: A Biography of David Lipscomb* (Nashville: David Lipscomb College, 1979), 72.

6 Peter Brock, *Pacifism in the United States: From the Colonial Era to the First World War* (Princeton: Princeton University Press, 1968), 911-915. A basic survey of attitudes towards war in American religious history is Alan Johnson, "The Bible and War in America: An Historical Survey," *Journal of the Evangelical Theological Society* 28

(June 1985), 169-181.

7 The pacifism of the NBST was not monolithic. Lipscomb and Harding were absolutists, believing that Christians should not even vote. R. H. Boll held an evolving vision. Deeply committed to peace and opposed to war, he nonetheless came to embrace a position that allowed a chastened allegiance to one's country. Cf. Michael W. Casey, "Neither Militant nor Pacifist: R. H. Boll on War and Peace" unpublished paper delivered to the 1998 Christian Scholar Conference at Pepperdine University.

8 Lipscomb, "Notes on Politics and Voting," *GA* 18 (8 June 1876), 544.

9 Lipscomb, *CG*, 131.

10 Lipscomb, "America and War," *GA* 18 (17 February 1876), 166.

11 Lipscomb, *CG*, 57.

12 L. C. Sears, *For Freedom: The Biography of John Nelson Armstrong* (Austin, TX: Sweet Publishing, 1969), 28, 35.

13 Lipscomb, *CG*, 64.

14 Michael W. Casey and Michael A. Jordan, "Free Speech in Time of War: Government Surveillance of the Churches of Christ in World War I," *Free Speech Yearbook* 34 (1996), 103.

15 Information on the Espionage Act of 1917 is available at http://en.wikipedia.org/wiki/Espionage_Act and the Sedition Act of 1918 at http://en.wikipedia.org/wiki/Sedition_Act_of_1918

16 Michael W. Casey, "The Closing of Cordell Christian College: A Microcosm of American Intolerance during World War I," *Chronicles of Oklahoma* 76 (Spring 1998), 24. We are dependant on this article for much of the information on Cordell Christian College.

17 Earl West, "World War I and the Decline of David Lipscomb's Civil Government," unpublished lecture delivered at the National Bicentennial Conference on "Alexander Campbell and the Spirit of the Revolution from Armagh to Bethany," at Bethany College, July 10, 1976, p. 11.

18 Casey, "Closing of Cordell Christian College," 29.

19 Sears, *For Freedom*, 158.

20 G. H. P. Showalter, "So-Called Conscientious Objectors," *FF* (18 June 1918), 3.

21 Quoted in Michael W. Casey, "From Pacifism to Patriotism: The Emergence of Civil Religion in Churches of Christ During World War I," *Mennonite Quarterly Review* 66 (July 1992), 386.

22 J. C. McQuiddy, "Conscientious Objectors," *GA* 59 (26 July 1917), 720-721. J. N. Armstrong was critical of McQuiddy's surrender to government pressure. In Armstrong's opinion McQuiddy "never accepted the antiwar position for

Christians," cf. "J. C. McQuiddy's Course and F. W. Smith's Complaint," *GA* 62 (9 December 1920), 1190-1191. Armstrong also states that twelve or more members of the Church of Christ had been sentenced to "twenty years' imprisonment because of their consciences."

23 For more on Whiteside's rejection of pacifism, see Robert P. Valentine, "Robertson Lafayette Whiteside: Systematic Theologian for the Churches of Christ" (unpublished Guided Research Paper, Harding Graduate School of Religion, 2001), pp. 86-96.

24 Whiteside, "What About Your War Record?" *GA* 62 (28 October 1920), 1048.

25 Whiteside, "Queries and Answers: Christians Duty as to War," *GA* 78 (18 June 1936), 585.

26 Whiteside as quoted in Foy E. Wallace Jr., *The Christian and the Government* (Nashville: Foy E. Wallace, Jr. Publications, 1968), 67.

27 H. Leo Boles, "Christian Nonresistance," *GA* 78 (18 June 1936), 602. Boles entered NBS in 1903 and served as President twice, 1913-1920 and 1923-1932.

28 Whiteside, "Concerning War," *Bible Banner* 5 (June 1943), 1.

29 Wallace, "The Lipscomb Theory of Civil Government," *Bible Banner* 6 (October 1943), 6.

30 Lipscomb, "God Uses the Evil as Well as the Good," *GA* 22 (30 September 1880), 634.

31 See Peter C. Craigie, *The Problem of War in the Old Testament* (Grand Rapids: Eerdmans, 1978).

32 Moses Lard, one of the few Stone-Campbell preachers to wrestle with the problem of war in the Old Testament, concluded that there is no precedent in these wars for modern warfare. "Jewish Wars as Precedents for Modern Wars," *Lard's Quarterly* 5 (April 1868), 113-126.

33 Craigie, *The Problem of War*, 83-91.

34 Richard B. Hays, *The Moral Vision of the New Testament: A Contemporary Introduction to New Testament Ethics* (San Francisco: Harper Collins, 1996), 322.

35 Ibid., 331. John Howard Yoder has demonstrated that Romans 13 must be understood in the wider context of the epistle. The passage, in context, does not negate our argument. Cf. *The Politics of Jesus* (Grand Rapids: Eerdmans, 1972), 193-214.

36 Or, as Yoder puts it, "The believing community is the new world on the way." *For the Nations: Essays Public & Evangelical* (Grand Rapids: Eerdmans, 1997), 50.

37 Lipscomb, *CG,* 135.

38 Lipscomb, "Notes on Politics and Voting," *GA* 18 (8 June 1876), 545.

39 Lee Camp, *Mere Discipleship: Radical Christianity in a Rebellious World*, (Grand

Rapids: Brazos Press, 2003), 145.

40 Ibid., 44.

41 Bartolome de Las Casas, *A Short Account of the Destruction of the Indies*, edited and translated by Nigel Griffin (New York: Penguin Books, 1992), 82

42 Ibid., 127.

43 Campbell, "Address on War."

44 Roland H. Bainton, *Christian Attitudes Toward War and Peace* (Nashville: Abingdon, 1960), 252-268.

45 Quoted in Yoder, *For the Nations*, 136.

46 Campbell, "Address on War."

CHAPTER TEN: NO CREED BUT CHRIST

1 John Rogers, "The Church of Christ at Concord, to the Elders and Brethren Assembled in Conference at Caneridge, Sendeth Christian Salutation," *Christian Messenger* 4 (October 1830), 258.

2 Quoted in L. C. Sears, *For Freedom: A Biography of John Nelson Armstrong* (Austin, TX: Sweet, 1969), 276.

3 Robert Hooper, *Crying in the Wilderness: A Biography of David Lipscomb* (Nashville: David Lipscomb College, 1979), 192. On Higbee see pp. 189 and 165.

4 Cf. C. Leonard Allen, *Things Unseen: Churches of Christ in (and After) the Modern Age* (Siloam Springs: Leafwood, 2004), 117-131. Some of Holman's writings are available at http://www.mun.ca/rels/restmov/people/sholman.html

5 *The New Testament Church: Editorials of F. D. Srygley Which Appeared in the Gospel Advocate from 1889 to 1900*, compiled and edited by F. B. Srygley (Nashville: Gospel Advocate, 1955), 194.

6 See especially Nathan Hatch, "The Christian Movement and the Demand for a Theology of the People," in *American Origins of Churches of Christ: Three Essays on Restoration History*, ed. Richard Hughes (Abilene, TX: ACU Press, 2000), 11-43.

7 Barton Stone, "Last Will and Testament of the Springfield Presbytery," in *Christian Documents Advocating Christian Union*, ed. C. A. Young, (Joplin, MO: College Press, 1985), 20.

8 Thomas Campbell, "Declaration and Address," in C. A. Young, *Christian Documents*, 71-72.

9 Lipscomb, "Queries on Civil Government," *GA* 17 (22 April 1875), 399-400.

10 R. L. Whiteside, "The Memory of Three Great Men," *Bible Banner* 6 (May 1944), 6.

11 James Challen, "The Millennium," *The Christian Quarterly* 6 (April 1874), 247-255; available at http://www.mun.ca/rels/restmov/texts/jchallen/themillennium.html

12 Moses Lard, "A Theory of the Millennium," *Lard's Quarterly* 2 (October 1864), 1-21; available at http://www.mun.ca/rels/restmov/texts/mlard/lard1.html

13 T. W. Brents, "The Millennium," in *Gospel Sermons* (Nashville: McQuiddy Printing, 1915), 324-352

14 Kevin James Gilbert, The Stone-Campbell Millennium: A Historical-Theological Perspective" *RQ* 43 (2001), 33-50; available at http://www.restorationquarterly.org/Volume_043/rq04301gilbert.htm Cf. James Stephen Wolfgang, "Millennial Themes in the Restoration Movement, Civil War to 1900," *Discipliana* 62 (Winter 2002), 99-115.

15 There had never been a uniform approach to the interpretation of the Apocalypse. See M. Eugene Boring, "Disciples Interpretation of Revelation at the Turn of the Century," *Discipliana* 59 (Fall 1999), 67-81;

16 Quoted in Douglas A. Foster, "Sectarian Strife in the Midst of the Fundamentalist-Modernist Crises: The Premillennial Controversy in the Churches of Christ" (unpublished paper delivered at the conference on Methodism and the Fragmentation of American Protestantism, 1865-1920: Papers from the Wesleyan-Holiness Studies Center Conference, Sept. 29-30, 1995), p. 18.

17 Letter, R. H. Boll, Louisville, Kentucky to A.B. Lipscomb, December 2, 1915. Center for Restoration Studies, Abilene Christian University.

18 Sears, *For Freedom*, 176.

19 J. N. Armstrong to John T. Lewis, Birmingham, Alabama, letter located in the J. D. Bales materials at Harding University Brackett Library. Though undated, the letter mentions an article by Armstrong published in 1935 and probably was written about that time.

20 E. M. Borden, "Brother Armstrong Concerning Brother Boll," *Herald of Truth* 4 (6 November 1924), 1-2.

21 Sears, *For Freedom*, 172.

22 Quoted in J. N. Armstrong, "My Open Letter to Brother Borden," *Living Message* 2 (13 November 1924), 527.

23 Ibid., 528.

24 Ibid., 525.

25 Sears, *For Freedom*, 185.

26 Armstrong, "We Regard too Lightly the Causing of Division," *Living Message* 3 (19 February 1925), 117. Cf. "Unity Required by the New Testament," *Living Message* 3 (19 March 1925), 178-179.

27 Armstrong, "We Regard too Lightly the Causing of Division," 118.

28 R. L. Whiteside and C. R. Nichol, *Christ and His Kingdom* (Clifton, TX: Mrs. C. R. Nichol Publisher, 1925). The book was widely received in Churches of Christ. Cf. D. S. Draper, "Two Books," *FF* 42 (27 October 1925), 7; F. B. Srygley,

"Commendation," *GA* 67 (4 June 1925), 534; F. W. Smith, "Boll's Doctrine Reviewed," *GA* 67 (21 May 1925), 485; J. S. Newman, "A Review," *FF* 42 (27 October 1925), 7; Unsigned, "Debate on the Kingdom," *CL* 39 (12 May 1925), 7; endorsements include N. B. Hardeman, Will W. Slater and C. E. Woolridge, "Review of R. H. Boll," *FF* 42 (8 December 1925), 5.

29 Whiteside and Nichol, *Christ and His Kingdom*, 72.

30 Ibid., 27.

31 Armstrong, "Random Remarks," *Living Message* 3 (23 July 1925), 468.

32 R. H. Boll, "A Statement," *WW* 28 (November 1935), 209.

33 Richard T. Hughes, *Reviving the Ancient Faith: The Story of Churches of Christ in America* (Grand Rapids: Eerdmans, 1996), 161-162.

34 F. F. Bruce, *Paul: Apostle of the Heart Set Free* (Grand Rapids: Eerdmans, 1978).

35 Eugene Peterson, *Traveling Light: Modern Meditations on St. Paul's Letter of Freedom* (Colorado Springs: Helmers & Howard, 1988), 57.

36 Quoted in Peterson, *Traveling Light*, 149.

37 R. H. Boll, "The Letter and the Spirit," *LM* 2 (30 October 1924), 494-495.

38 R. H. Boll, "The Secret of Joyless Christian Lives," *GA* 52 (17 March 1910), 322. Cf. "Babes and Hypocrites," *The Way* 3 (25 April 1901), 25-27.

39 Alexander Campbell, "To an Independent Baptist," *Christian Baptist* 3 (1 May 1826), 237.

CHAPTER ELEVEN: NO MORE SHADOWS

1 Harding, "For What Are We Here?" *The Way* 5 (3 December 1903), 1041.

2 Cf. Richard T. Hughes, *Reviving the Ancient Faith* (Grand Rapids: Eerdmans, 1996), 137-167.

3 Cf. Kevin James Gilbert, "The Stone-Campbell Millennium: A Historical Theological Perspective," *RQ* 43.1 (2001), 33-50.

4 R. C. Bell claimed he taught it "with both tongue and pen" (as quoted by Kenneth Wayne Green, "The Life and Times of James A. Harding," [M.A. Thesis, Abilene Christian College, 1960], 123). E. L. Jorgenson, a leader among premillennial Churches of Christ, claimed that the first sermon he ever heard Harding preach was entitled "The Millennium" and it "sank deep into my heart and mind" (E. L. Jorgenson, *Faith of Our Fathers* [Louisville, KY: Word and Work Publishers, n.d.], 309).

5 "I do not find enough concerning the matter to fix my faith one way or the other," Lipscomb wrote in answer to a query. "I am no interpreter of unexplained prophecy" (*QA, 516).* Queried about the Millennium, Lipscomb answered: "The best way to bring about the millennium is to teach and practice obedience to the practical precepts for the Bible. Practice the precepts and follow the example of the Savior, and this will do a thousandfold more to fully bring about the reign of Jesus

on earth than a thousand discourses and theories about what the millennium is or when it begins or ends" (Lipscomb, "Queries," *GA* 42 [23 June 1898], 397).

6 As quoted by Kenneth Wayne Green, "The Life and Times of James A. Harding" (M.A. Thesis, Abilene Christian College, 1960), 123.

7 *Q&A*, 360.

8 *CG*, 13.

9 Harding, "For What Are We Here?" *CLW* 5 (3 December 1903), 1041.

10 Harding, "Man Was Created to Reign for Ever and Ever," *CLW* 19 (6 June 1905), 8.

11 Harding, "The Kingdom of Christ Vs. the Kingdom of Satan," *CLW* 5 (15 October 1903), 930.

12 Ibid.

13 Harding, "The Holy Spirit — A Bible Reading," *The Way* 1 (1 August 1899), 114-8; *CLW* 18 (31 May 31 1904), 8-9 and 18 (7 June 1904), 8-9; and *GH* 1 (29 May 1913), 1.

14 Harding, "The Holy Spirit in the Church," 8.

15 Harding, "The Gift of the Holy Spirit. A Reply to Dr. Holloway," 8.

16 Ibid.

17 Harding, "Man Was Created to Reign for Ever and Ever," *CLW* 19 (6 June 1905), 8.

18 Harding, "Scraps," *The Way* 4 (22 May 1902), 57.

19 Harding, "Kingdom," 930.

20 Ibid, 930.

21 Harding, "Man was Created," 8.

22 Harding, "Kingdom," 930-1.

23 Harding, "Scraps," *The Way* 4 (17 April 1902), 17.

24 Harding, "Scraps," *The Way* 4 (22 May 1902), 57.

25 Harding, "For What Are We Here?" 1042.

26 Harding, "Scraps," *The Way* 4 (17 April 1902), 17.

27 Harding, "Man was Created," 8.

28 Harding, "Scraps," *The Way* 4 (17 April 1902), 17.

29 Anthony Hoekema, *The Bible and the Future* (Grand Rapids: Eerdmans, 1979), 280-81.

30 Some read "melt" in 2 Peter 3:12 literally while others metaphorically as apocalyptic imagery much like Isaiah 34:4 or Micah 1:4. Given the parallel with Noah, it is best to read it as an apocalyptic metaphor. Just as Noah's world was destroyed, then renewed, so the coming fire will destroy the world and renewal will follow.

31 Cf. Walter Brueggemann, "The Hope of Heaven…On Earth," *Biblical Theology Bulletin* 29 (Fall 1999), 99-111.

32 Lipscomb, "The Kingdom of God," 328

33 Harding, "The Second Coming of Jesus—When Will it Be?" *The Way* 4 (25 September 1902), 203-4.

34 Ibid., 203.

35 Boll, "Hastening the Day," *GA* 52 (10 November 1910), 1226: "The plans and purpose of God, though in the end never thwarted, can be hastened and delayed...If, then, it is the sign of the consummation of the age that the gospel of the kingdom should be preached to all nations for a testimony unto them, and then shall come the end-let us do all we can to speed and further God's great work, and to hasten the day according to his will. Aside from the love of souls which is characteristic of the Christian mind, aside from the obedience to Christ's commission-her is a motive for world-wide missions."

36 Maltbie D. Babcock, "This is My Father's World," lyrics available at http://www.higherpraise.com/Lyrics4/ThisIsMyFathersWorld.htm.

CHAPTER TWELVE: THE ROAD NOT TRAVELED

1 R. H. Boll, "Christian Nations," *WW* 9 (February 1916), 51

2 C. Leonard Allen, Richard T. Hughes, and Michael R. Weed, *The Worldly Church: A Call to Biblical Renewal,* 2nd Edition (Abilene, TX: ACU Press, 1991).

3 Richard T. Hughes, *Reviving the Ancient Faith: The Story of Churches of Christ in America* (Grand Rapids: Eerdmans, 1966), 47-134.

4 C. Leonard Allen, *Things Unseen: Churches of Christ in (After After) the Modern Age* (Siloam Springs, AR: Leafwood Publishers, 2004), 71-98.

5 Hughes, *Reviving the Ancient Faith*, 137-189; Robert E. Hooper, *A Distinct People: A History of Churches of Christ in the 20th Century* (West Monroe: Howard Publishing Co., 1993), 131-156.

6 Walter Brueggemann, *Texts Under Negotiation: The Bible and Postmodern Imagination* (Minneapolis: Fortress Press, 1993), 26-56.

7 Stephen R. Holmes, *Listening to the Past: The Place of Tradition in Theology* (Grand Rapids: Baker Academic, 2002), especially 18-36.